Confessions
from the Far Side
of Thirty

Confessions from the Far Side of Thirty

Kathi Mills

VICTOR BOOKS

A DIVISION OF SCRIPTURE PRESS PUBLICATIONS INC.
USA CANADA ENGLAND

All Scripture is from *The New King James Version.*
© 1979, 1980, 1982, Thomas Nelson, Inc.,
Publishers. Used by permission.

Copyediting: Barbara Williams
Cover Design: Scott Rattray
Cover Illustration: Paul Blumstein

Library of Congress Cataloging-in-Publication Data

Mills, Kathi, 1948-

Confessions from the far side of thirty / by Kathi Mills.

p.   cm.

ISBN 1-56476-095-2

1. Middle aged women—Religious life. 2. Mills, Kathi, 1948- .
3. Christian life—   1960-   I. Title.

BV4579.5.M55   1993

248.8′43–dc20   92-37774

                                                                        CIP

1 2 3 4 5 6 7 8 9 10   Printing/Year 97 96 95 94 93

To all the "little people"
who make me what I am today —
a grandma!

— Shana, Adam, Mikey,
Karissa, Neeco, Brittney —

I love you all!

CONTENTS

When was the last time you actually looked forward to your next birthday? Come on, be honest. It's been awhile, right? But no matter how many years your "awhile" entails, I imagine I'm safe in assuming you were still young then. *Very young.* Like, under twenty-five. And then it happened. You woke up one morning, looked in the mirror, and gasped, "Thirty? Me? Impossible!" But it was true. And things have never been the same since.

In a world where the "beautiful people" are never over thirty—and if they are, they certainly don't look it—it's tough to compete. Impossible, in fact, as the years sail by faster and faster, taking their inevitable toll.

But who says we have to compete? And exactly what is it we're competing for? While I don't advocate folding our tents and silently slipping off into the sunset at the first sign of gray hair and crow's feet, must we become obsessed with preventing waistline spread and thunder thighs? Must we dedicate our very beings to a never-ending crusade to discover new and more efficient ways to ingest fiber into our systems? Or is it just remotely possible that there really is life after cellulite?

I truly wish I could answer that last question with a resounding "Yes!" But you see, I too have long since said good-bye to thirty-anything, and like so many others in my age bracket (the first of us baby boomers to find ourselves in the grip of middle-aged maladies), I constantly vacillate between acceptance and downright rage.

I know, I know. A mature person with a strong self-image — particularly a Christian who can quote countless Scriptures about the wisdom and respect that comes with old age, not to mention the relative unimportance of this present life in relation to the eternal hereafter — should be able to accept the inevitable progression from youth to middle-age to senior citizenship with anticipation and joy. Or, at the very least, with a certain amount of dignity and decorum. At times, I manage to do so. At other times, however, I find myself trying to choose between taking out a second mortgage on the house so I can go to the nearest plastic surgeon for a face (and body) lift, or just sitting down and laughing at the absurdity of it all. So far, I've been able to restrain myself and opt for the laughing. And you know what? By the time I'm through laughing, I usually find that things have somehow fallen into perspective once more, and I've actually learned something in the process—something that just might be worth passing along to someone else. Hence, *Confessions from the Far Side of Thirty.*

Now, I can't promise that this collection of insights, gathered from the everyday experiences of a woman who has made a career out of never taking anyone's word for anything, but rather learning it all the hard way (my husband says he has no problem whatsoever believing that I am directly descended from the stiff-necked Israelites), will make you start looking forward to birthdays once again. But if it gives you a few laughs—and maybe even a greater appreciation for God's limitless grace—along the way, it was well worth the writing.

Besides, what have you got to lose? The Bible says, "A merry heart does good, like medicine" (Prov. 17:22). And at our age, I figure we need all the help we can get.

15

HOW DO YOU DO?
I DON'T SPEAK ENGLISH

WHEN WE WERE FIRST ASKED to host a foreign exchange student, I had my reservations. This student was a teenager, and what kind of people willingly invite another teenager into their home?

And yet, the more we talked about it, the more we sensed that it might be an excellent learning experience for all of us—especially the one teenager of our own who was still living at home.

The day the students were to arrive, I found myself to be the one elected to pick up our new boarder, simply because my husband was at work and my son had taken off that morning with a banana in one hand and a basketball in the other. I hadn't seen him since.

Oh, well, I reasoned. How hard can it be to drive

17

down to the school parking lot and wait for the bus to arrive from the airport? After all, we already knew his name was Susumu; I would simply hold up a sign with his name on it. And the woman who approved our application had told me that Susumu spoke some English, so no problem, right?

Wrong. As soon as the bus pulled up, about 5,000 tired, hungry, nervous Japanese teenagers piled off, looking around anxiously for their new "families." Susumu saw my sign, walked toward me, handed me a Japanese dictionary, and then announced, "How do you do? I don't speak English."

That was it. His entire English vocabulary in five seconds. Those eight words were the "some English" I had been told he spoke. Of course, it was eight more words than I knew in Japanese, so we were off to a real good start.

Well, I managed to get Susumu and his suitcases loaded into the car, and off we went to what would be Susumu's home for the next six weeks. We spent the first hour working out the basics, like, "This is your room. This is the bathroom. This is the kitchen." The entire time, he followed me dutifully from room to room, nodding and smiling, obviously wondering what in the world I was talking about and why he'd ever decided to make this trip in the first place.

All along I was chalking all this up to a cultural and language barrier, but then my son got home. Chris was less than a year younger than Susumu, so he motioned Susumu to follow him into his room. When they emerged soon after, Chris informed me that Susumu needed to call his parents to let them know he had arrived safely, that cantaloupes cost $5 each in Japan, and that Susumu hadn't slept in almost forty-eight hours.

That's when I understood that the problem was not a language barrier, but a generation gap. Once again, I'd been put in my place — middle-age. Teenagers could somehow communicate with each other without words, even though few of them have ever been known to say anything intelligible to adults. I, however, could communicate no better with a foreign teenager (is there any other kind?) than I could with my own.

Somehow though, we all managed to make it through the next six weeks without any major mishaps. I even learned a few words in Japanese (practical things, like how to say "chair," "dog," "fork," and "umbrella," all of which I have since forgotten), while Susumu was conversing in full sentences by the time he left.

Yet, in spite of our communication problems, it didn't take long for Susumu to fit right into the family. In fact, it seemed we were developing our very own language — the language of love.

Which, I have decided, is how it will be in heaven. There will be no language barriers — or generation gaps — there. Because we will be living in the very presence of love Himself, we will all be able to communicate with one another in the language of love, no matter what language we may have spoken here on earth.

I find this to be a comforting thought, because now I know I won't arrive in heaven, only to be met at the bus by someone who says, "How do you do? I don't speak English."

Instead, I will hear those wonderful words, "Welcome. Come and join us. The family's been waiting."

Thanks, Susumu. You may not have spoken much English, but you taught me a lot about communication.

THAT'S ENTERTAINMENT?

I REMEMBER SO WELL, lying across my bed, staring starry-eyed at my poster of Elvis Presley, while playing and replaying such romantic classics as "Hound Dog" and "Jailhouse Rock."

I can also remember my mother coming to my bedroom door and asking, "Dear, could you turn that down a bit, please?" Eighteen renditions of "Don't Be Cruel" later, her tone began to change—definitely not for the better. "Shouldn't you be doing your homework instead of wasting your time listening to that . . . music?"

I would then explain that I was doing my homework while I listened. The only reason it didn't appear that I was getting anything accomplished was that I was still in the "thinking stages," but I was getting ready to start the reading and writing part any minute.

By the time I was dreaming my way through "Blue Hawaii," her voice had risen to a feverish pitch. "If I hear one more Elvis Presley song today I'm going to scream!" (I thought that's what she was already doing.) However, because I loved my mother and knew she had a problem with high blood pressure (not to mention the fact that I had just decided to stop listening to records and go to my friend's house), I obediently turned off my record player.

Have you ever noticed how history has a way of repeating itself? I cannot tell you the times I have gone to my teenager's bedroom door and threatened him with annihilation "if you don't turn that thing off right now!"

"That thing," however, is not what could, in any way, be equated with the record player I had when I was his age. No, "that thing" has more buttons and switches and modules and dials than a nuclear submarine. It's a good thing he's never figured out that I couldn't turn it off if my life depended on it or I'd be totally at his mercy. (What a chilling thought!)

However, record players aren't the only pieces of entertainment equipment that have evolved into complicated mechanisms over the years. Have you tried to buy a new TV lately?

My husband and I went looking for one a few years ago because the one we had was so old we could no longer find anyone to work on it. I was all for tossing it and putting a planter in its place, but I was outvoted, so we went TV shopping.

"I assume you're interested in Dolby and Stadium Surround?" the salesman asked, as we stood staring at 493 TVs, all showing a color special on the almost extinct African penguin.

My husband looked at me as if I should know what the man was talking about. I smiled. "We really don't have a brand in mind," I explained. "Although we've been real happy with our old Emerson. You wouldn't happen to have any of their new models on hand, would you?"

The salesman (who looked like he had just graduated from high school earlier that month) stared at me blankly. "Excuse me?" he said.

By the time we got our new TV home (I think it's made by Dolby Surround, which I assume is a new nationwide company), we had also bought a complicated remote control to go with it. ("So you won't have to get up and down to change channels," the salesman explained.)

Well, he was wrong about that. After several months of trying to figure that thing out, we gave up. But we have learned how to manually turn our Dolby Surround TV on and off, as well as change the channels. And, as far as getting up and down to walk to the TV, we figure we need all the exercise we can get, right?

Besides, after seeing the quality of what's on TV most of the time (I guarantee you, our old Emerson got a lot better programs), we've decided that watching each other walk back and forth is a lot more entertaining than any of the so-called "prime-time specials."

There's no doubt about it. Entertainment has changed. And not for the better. Is it really a coincidence that the morals of this country have declined proportionately with the declining morals of the entertainment industry? I think not.

The scary thing is, many of us who call ourselves Christians also listen to and/or watch this junk.

Maybe it's time we started measuring what we allow into our minds against Philippians 4:8, which tells us to think on things that are true, noble, just, pure, lovely, of good report, virtuous, and praiseworthy. Doesn't sound like many TV programs I've seen on our Dolby lately.

Because, although times have changed, God's standards for His children have not.

KEEPING UP WITH
THE LATEST FASHIONS

I HAVE TO ADMIT, I don't always keep up with the latest fashions, for the plain and simple reason that I think most of them are downright ugly. But I do get a kick out of seeing who the infamous "they" decide are the year's best and worst dressed celebrities.

Oh, don't worry, I don't waste my hard-earned money on those sleazy magazines that tell all about the love lives of the rich and famous. I don't have to. I simply read the headlines while I'm waiting in line at the checkout counter at the grocery store. (You know, headlines like "Two-Headed Chicken Lays Double-Yoked Egg" and "Is Saddam Hussein Really Elvis Presley in Disguise?")

The trouble is, even when they have the pictures

of the best and worst dressed celebrities on the magazine cover, I still have a hard time deciding who's who. Is the woman wearing the skin-tight, black sequined, feather-covered dress accentuated by scuffed combat boots and a baseball cap one of the best or the worst? Either way, I'd rather wear a sweatsuit.

Let's face it. Fashions change as fast, or faster, than the times. And, even though we tried our best to keep up with the latest fads when we were young, have you noticed that, somewhere we hit a point where we just plain got stuck?

Fortunately for me, it wasn't when bell-bottoms or miniskirts were the rage. But I have noticed that my wardrobe does tend to date me as having given up on fashion about ten years ago.

Of course, I suppose I can be glad that, even though I may be one of the older baby boomers, I at least escaped the age where those slightly older than I got stuck in polyester. You know what I mean. That wonder material that washes and wears, never needs ironing, and never, ever wears out. It's also cheap because no one under Social Security age would be caught dead in it.

You have to admit, though, it does travel well. Polyester wouldn't wrinkle if you crumpled it up and sat on it (which isn't a bad idea). Best of all, those who wear it don't see anything wrong with it because everyone else they hang out with wears it also. Birds of a feather, right?

Then again, maybe those folks have lived long enough that they no longer feel the need to prove anything to anyone. Comfort and practicality have long since taken precedence over fashion. Whereas the younger generation is still trying to make a statement of individuality through their clothes — not realizing, of course, that in doing so, they all look exactly alike.

I suppose we baby boomers are somewhere in between. Most of us have settled into families, careers, lifestyles, and so have quit trying to express the outrageous or bizarre in our choice of clothes. At the same time, we aren't quite at the point where we don't care about what anybody thinks so let's throw out the ironing board, head to K Mart, and scoop up a rack of polyester.

But just what kind of a fashion statement are we making? Does the way we dress say, "I'm successful and important and you better pay attention to me?" Does it scream out that we, like our younger counterparts, are still searching for . . . something? Does it whisper, like the polyester generation, that we have already given up?

Or does it honor the One we claim to love and serve? Does it say that we care enough about ourselves — regardless of our age — to take the time to make a good impression, whatever style of clothing we select, while at the same time proclaiming that current fads in fashion do not dictate our standards, nor are we trying to compete with those best and worst dressed celebrities who beckon to us from the grocery store checkout stands?

Because when it's all said and done, that's exactly what it will be — said and done. No more grocery store checkout stands, no more best and worst dressed celebrities, no more polyester or black sequins. There will be no one left to impress — except our Heavenly Father. And the only thing He wants to see us dressed in is a robe of righteousness.

Have you got yours? If not, Jesus has one with your name on it — and it's just your size.

FIRST AND TEN...
DO IT AGAIN?

ALL RIGHT. I ADMIT IT. I haven't always been a sports fan. In fact, when I decided as a teenager to try out for cheerleader, it had nothing at all to do with a love for sports. I just wanted to wear one of those cute little skirts and a sweater with a letter on the front. (Have you noticed that cheerleading outfits are one of the few styles that haven't changed since the last generation?)

To tell you the truth, I went through my entire cheerleading career not knowing whether to yell, "First and ten . . . do it again" or "Hold that line." I didn't know a lay-up from a free throw, a touchback from a touchdown. And, frankly, I didn't care.

But all that changed in the summer of 1982

when my husband, Larry, came home and excited-
ly announced, "Guess what? I just got season tickets for the Raiders' first year at the Coliseum!"

"That's nice," I remarked, standing over the
sink while I peeled potatoes for dinner. Then,
without even looking up, I asked, "How much did
they cost?"

"Three hundred and sixty dollars."

I almost amputated my thumb. "What?" I cried,
whirling to face him. "You paid almost $400 so
you could drive all the way to L.A. and watch a
bunch of guys jump on each other and fight over a
stupid little ball?"

"Oh, not just for me," he went on, smiling ex-
pectantly. "The tickets are for you too."

Now there's one thing you have to understand
about me. As any and all who know me will attest,
I never do anything halfway. So, when my husband
dragged me to the Coliseum for the first season
game, I demanded a complete explanation for every play, every call, every change on the score-
board. I studied the program until I knew the
players' names and stats and positions by heart. By
the end of the game, my old cheerleader training

31

must have surfaced, because I was jumping up and down and screaming so loudly that my poor husband was beginning to get embarrassed.

I, of course, wasn't embarrassed—just pleasantly surprised that I still had enough energy at my age to do that sort of thing—and amazed to discover that I had fallen in love with the game of football. From that day on, I lived and breathed football. I read everything I could find about the game, the players, the coaches. I learned which teams were running teams, which ones were passing teams, who was being traded to whom, and how those trades would affect the teams' futures. After spending all day Saturday watching college games and all day Sunday as well as Monday evening watching pro games, I would get up early the next morning and breathlessly await the arrival of the *Los Angeles Times* so I could relive the games in print.

Then it happened. My first January as a football fan. The Rose Bowl, the Orange Bowl, the Super Bowl! Could life possibly get any better?

But wait! How could this be? I came home from church the Sunday after the Pro Bowl, flipped on the TV, and — there was no football! Frantically, I grabbed the paper and scanned the TV listings. Nothing!

"No more football," my husband explained. "Not until next season — the end of summer."

The end of summer! How would I survive? What would I do?

"There's always basketball," Larry suggested. "The Lakers are a great team, you know."

The Lakers. Yeah, I'd heard of them. Some big guy named Kareem something-or-other. Well, why not? I had to find some way of keeping myself from falling into a six-month depression.

Did it work? Well, suffice it to say that, a few years later when my first book was published, I skipped an autograph party because it coincided with a crucial Laker/Jazz playoff game. A couple of weeks after that, at a dinner to honor local women authors, I sat huddled in a corner chair, dressed to the teeth and trying to look inconspicuous as I held my tiny transistor radio to my ear. Even then, I managed to control myself — until the end of the game, that is, when my beloved Los Angeles Lakers defeated the Detroit Pistons in a seventh and final playoff game, making the Lakers back-to-back champions of the NBA.

I will probably never again be allowed in that restaurant (I jumped so high, Michael "Air" Jordan would have been proud of me, and when I screamed, the busboy dropped a trayful of 18 water-filled glasses on the table in front of the guest of honor), but there are few times in my life that compare with the ecstasy I felt at that moment.

So, it wasn't too surprising when I grabbed the chance to work with former football great Rosey Grier on a book about famous Christian athletes. The testimony of each athlete we interviewed was a true source of inspiration for me. And I discovered that, though their stories were all different, the message was the same: the striving for excellence, the level of personal commitment that made each of those athletes great in his or her field, was reflected in a personal commitment to Jesus Christ. I was also impressed with their messages of love — love for God, for family, for friends, and yes, love for sports.

But the love that flowed so freely from those committed athletes was a love that helped keep everything in perspective — even for "fanatics" like myself. It is a love that is not afraid to stand up and declare that all the honors, all the trophies, all the accolades the world has to offer can never compare to the joy and fulfillment that can come only from being truly loved and forgiven, from knowing and fellowshiping with the very God of the universe.

It's enough to make even middle-aged cheerleaders like me jump up and down and shout in triumph!

Adapted from *Winning* by Rosey Grier and Kathi Mills (Ventura, Calif.: Regal Books, 1990). Used by permission.

HAVE YOU FORMATTED YOUR FLOPPY TODAY?

DIRECTIONS CONFUSE ME. They irritate me. They intimidate me. At times, they terrify me. Consequently, I tend to ignore them and just muddle through the best way I can. Which, the vast majority of the time, proves to be my undoing.

Nothing illustrates this fact better than the time I finally caved in to everyone's advice that, if I was going to have any sort of success as a writer, I simply *had* to have a personal computer. (So how come all those great "Murder, She Wrote" mysteries get written on that ancient machine I see on TV?)

However, after enduring countless accusations of being a dinosaur, I gave in—but not without more than a tad bit of apprehension. I knew there wasn't a chance in the world that this brand-new wonder machine of mine was going to spring to life of its own accord. No, experience had taught me that it was going to arrive with its very own complicated set of directions.

I was right — almost. It didn't just arrive with one set of complicated directions — there were three sets! Three manuals, to be exact. And each one was labeled "Read me first."

Now, in addition to the fact that these manuals were obviously written by a foreign exchange student with absolutely no knowledge of the average, everyday personal computer user's limited direction-deciphering capabilities, the diagrams in the manuals did not match up with the computer they had sent me. In other words, they were definitely not user-friendly.

But, eventually, with the help of a friend who had a similar computer, I learned how to turn my computer on, how to enter the word processing part of my computer, how to use the keyboard in a relatively competent manner, and then how to exit the word processor and turn the computer off.

Not bad, right? (Of course, we won't even talk about the other 99 percent of my computer's functions, of which I have never availed myself.) The problem was, the first time I finished working on a story to send to a magazine, the editor asked me to send my material on "hard copy and disk."

"Sure," I answered. "No problem."

I hung up the phone and got out the trusty manuals and spent the next three hours trying to figure out just what it was the editor wanted. I figured it probably had something to do with my manuscript, but I wasn't even positive of that.

Frustrated, I called my friend, the one with a computer similar to mine. He was out of town for two weeks. So, in desperation, I called the store where I had purchased the computer. Not wanting to sound completely illiterate, I decided to use the tried-and-true approach of bluffing.

"Uh, I just finished writing a story for this magazine," I explained. "And they asked me to send them a hard copy and a disk."

Finally, the voice on the other end asked, "And?"

"And, um, well, it's the first assignment I've done on my new computer and—"

"What model is it?" asked the voice.

"Huh? Oh, well, I, uh . . . " I looked at the front

of my computer, hoping the model name and/or number would be there.

"Uh, Leading Edge," I informed him, reading the little logo below the screen.

"I see," he said. "But which model?"

I snatched up my direction manuals and began to paw through them. Nothing. *Stall him,* I thought.

"I, uh. . . . "

About that time, he must have figured out that he was talking with a total incompetent, because I could hear him swallow a chuckle as he said, "Why don't you tell me your name, and I'll go pull your records."

I considered changing my name, but decided that honesty was the only way I was ever going to find out what my editor wanted from me. So I told him. In no time, he was back with the information he needed to walk me through my immediate problem.

"OK," he began. "You say you've already completed the writing?"

I nodded, then realized he couldn't hear my head rattling. "Uh, yes," I answered, wondering if he thought I wrote for *Moron Monthly.* "Yes, I did."

"Do you have the copy off your printer yet?"

The light came on. Hard copy! What the editor wanted was the manuscript itself—on paper! OK, I could do that. Now, for the disk part.

"Yes," I answered. "Yes, I've run that off. But he also wants a disk."

"No problem," he said. (*Easy for him to say,* I thought.) "The first thing you have to do is format your floppy."

So much for progress. I was back to square one—or worse! At least before, all I needed was hard copy and a disk. Now I needed a floppy—and a formatted one, at that. I decided I could probably resell my computer right away without taking too big a loss. Then, if all went well, I could go to a secondhand store and find a typewriter like the "Murder, She Wrote" author had.

Well, thankfully, the man on the other end of the phone was very patient and, together, we eventually got my floppy formatted and my manuscript recorded and ready to mail. In spite of myself, I had just taken a major stride into the use of modern technology—with or without directions.

All of this gave me a better understanding of my German grandmother who, soon after her arrival in this country in 1948, was introduced to her first television set.

"I vill not haf one of dose in mine house," she announced. "If I can see dose peoples, dey can see me! Und I vill not haf peoples spying on me in mine own house!" And so my grandfather had to come to our house to watch wrestling.

My mother-in-law's logic isn't much different. For years, she had shopped at the same pharmacy—until she saw a sign in the window saying they had installed a FAX machine. "That's it," she said. "No more shopping there for me."

The reason? "FAX machines send things to other parts of the country, and I want to stay right here."

Sounds comical. But then, so does formatting your floppy, right? Times change and, in some cases anyway, we have to change with them. And it sure is a lot easier when we take the time to read (and follow) the directions.

That's what's wrong with our world today, you know. Not modern technology, but non-direction followers. God has given us all the directions we need to lead a joyful, peaceful, fulfilled life (as well as to get to heaven someday), but most people never take the time to read those directions. And, if they do, they throw up their hands in despair and claim that the Bible just doesn't make any sense.

Well, you know what? There is One who is the Recognized Expert on God's directions and who is just waiting—very, very patiently, I might add—to help explain those directions to anyone who will truthfully seek to understand them with all their heart. His name is Holy Spirit. His job is to come alongside us, to lead and guide us, to explain to us those directions that we do not understand.

If you've never met the Holy Spirit, that means you've never received Jesus Christ as your Lord and Savior. Do that right now, and the Holy Spirit will come to live inside you. Then you can commune with Him anytime, anywhere.

Go ahead. Get your direction manual out and give Him a call. He probably won't explain to you how to format your floppy, but He will walk you through the maze of everyday life as you make your way toward home.

And no matter about your learning rate, He will never put you on hold or hang up on you. I promise.

WHAT DOES A GRANDMA LOOK LIKE?

I WAS STILL IN MY THIRTIES when my first grandchild was born. And I have to admit, I loved hearing people say, "Why, you can't be a grandmother! You just don't look old enough."

Now that I have six grandchildren, however, people don't say that as often anymore. In fact, when I mention that I have six grandchildren, they say things like, "Oh, that's nice," or "I have eight." This tends to make me more than slightly suspicious that maybe I'm not holding my own as well as I thought I was.

And yet, let's be honest. Grandmas, along with the times, have changed. I never knew my maternal grandmother, who died when my mother was eight, but my father's mother, whom we affectionately called "Omi," was the light of my life.

Now Omi looked like a grandma. She was short, pulled her salt-and-pepper hair back into a bun at the nape of her neck, wore housedresses, aprons, and black platform shoes, and never showed up at our house without a coffee tin full of home-baked butter cookies.

My mom also became a respectable looking grandma, although in a different way from Omi. Mom was a bit taller than Omi, and her hair was much shorter. She gave up wearing housedresses when Harriet Nelson retired, she only occasionally wears aprons, and I have never seen her in plat-form shoes.

My youngest son, however, insists she is much more grandmotherly than I am because when he was little, he used to lean on her shoulder while she read to him. He brags about her as being "soft," but accuses me of having "bony shoul-ders" — obviously an automatic disqualification for a grandma position.

And I'll admit, my normal attire of blue jeans, shirts, and sandals doesn't do much to promote my grandma image. But then, I suppose what all this comes down to is—just what does a grandma look like anyway?

Well, thinking about all the grandmas I have ever known, I would have to say they are short, tall, fat, skinny, blonde, brunette, gray-headed, old, young, in-between, housewives, doctors, lawyers, truck drivers, politicians, American, Asian, African, European, tough, tender, soft, and even bony!

But inside, we're all the same. We have hearts that say, "I have survived motherhood, and now I'm going to take it easy and enjoy my grandchildren. If that includes a little spoiling, well, so be it. Whatever this job calls for, I will do it well."

Part of that job, of course, is to take a lot of pictures. All grandmas, whatever age, size, or shape, carry cameras with them at all times. I probably have a grand total of twenty-seven pictures of all my kids throughout their entire childhood. I have more than that of each of my grandchildren's first five minutes of life.

But back to the question: What does a grandma look like? Well, I must admit, that question is a little bit like another question I was asked not long ago: What does a Christian look like? I didn't have to think about that very long though, before I realized the only answer was, "A Christian looks like Jesus."

Now, accepting this statement means learning to walk by faith, and not by sight, since most of us, with the exception of some basic physical statistics, bear very little resemblance to Jesus Christ. But, according to 2 Corinthians 5:7, isn't walking by faith rather than by sight the way we're supposed to walk? If we allow ourselves to walk any other way, we will begin to judge and label people by their outward appearance, rather than by looking at their hearts, the way God does (see 1 Sam. 16:7).

I suppose then, that the answer to finding out what a grandma or a Christian or anyone else looks like is not to look at people at all, but to keep our eyes only on Jesus. When we do that, we will never go wrong. We will never lose our way. And we will never fail to recognize people for who they truly are.

COLOR ME GRAY

IT HAS ALWAYS AMAZED ME that people can find something good to say about the color gray. I mean, I can actually remember sitting in high school English, reading a poem that romanticized gray fog creeping in on cat's paws. (Out of respect for the writing profession, I will leave this deranged poet nameless.) Gimme a break! I don't care how poetic you are, gray is gray, and there's nothing romantic about it.

Of course, I suppose I should be perfectly honest here and admit that I never really thought muc about gray, one way or the other, until a few year ago when I looked into the mirror and ... ther it was. A gray hair. Neon gray, actually. Thic r, longer, and coarser than all the dark

47

ones, and sticking straight up in the air, taunting me like some macabre warning of things to come.

Well, my first thought upon seeing this unwelcome invader was to pull it right out. That was my second thought too, so I did. Then I wrapped it very carefully in aluminum foil and waited for my husband to come home.

"Look what I found today," I announced the moment he walked through the door.

He looked at my outstretched hand, then at me, puzzled. "Aluminum foil?" he asked.

"Not aluminum foil," I explained, lifting my hand higher so he could see the horror that lay, unbidden, in the middle of that unwrapped foil.

He looked back down at my hand, then shrugged. "I give up," he said. "Sure looks like aluminum foil to me."

Things were not going the way I'd planned. After waiting all day for him to come home so I could get a little sympathy and reassurance, all I got was a guy who'd obviously gone blind during the day and couldn't see the huge gray hair gleaming up at him.

"It's a gray hair," I cried, picking it up and holding it directly in front of his face.

"Oh," was all he said.

"It's mine," I explained.

"Oh."

"Oh?" I asked, incredulously. "That's all you can say! I've just shown you my first gray hair and all you can say is 'Oh'?"

The light seemed to dawn then as his puzzled frown turned into a mischievous grin. "Oh, now I get it," he said. "You're upset because this is your first gray hair."

(I guess we can all be glad he didn't become a psychiatrist, right?)

Anyway, he eventually figured out not only why I was upset, but why it would not be wise to tease me about it at that particular time. And, to be fair, he did try to comfort and reassure me. But it didn't work.

Every morning I'd jump out of bed and scrutinize my head in the mirror. Nothing. No more gray hairs. *A fluke*, I decided. *That's all it was, just a fluke. I probably won't get another one for years and years and. . . .*

And then one morning there were three of them.

All at once. No warning. Nothing. They just appeared out of nowhere. Sticking straight up. Gray. And I knew it was all over.

So I didn't even bother to pull them out. Instead, I got out my Bible and concordance and began looking up all the Scriptures I could find about gray hair. It was awesome! By the end of the day I was just about convinced that I was happy about my three gray hairs.

Just about, but not quite. So I decided to do what any normal, intelligent, fast-approaching-middle-age person would do—I colored my hair. For several years, in fact. Until one day not too long ago, just before it was time to color my hair again, when I looked in the mirror and realized that I liked the gray that was starting to show through. (I also realized that there were now too many gray hairs to count and/or pull out, so it was either continue to color them for the rest of my life, or accept them and grow old gracefully.)

Well, I'm happy to say that I have now stopped coloring my hair and have decided to wear my gray as a badge of courage—because, believe me, that's what it took to stop covering up the inevitable.

And, although I may not be ready to start writing poems about the beauty of gray fog and cat's paws, I am ready to move on into the next season of life, knowing that God's plans for me, whatever my age, are "of peace and not of evil, to give you a future and a hope" (Jer. 29:11).

I guess I just had to "grow up" a bit more before I could accept those plans and enjoy being colored gray.

ALL YOU EVER NEED
TO KNOW ABOUT LOVE

LOVE. WHAT KIND OF TOPIC IS THAT to bring up in a book for baby boomers? After all, we're supposed to be comfortably settled into at least the early stages of middle age by now, so what relevance could love have for old geezers like us? Well, since I happen to believe that love is ageless, that some things never change, and that some people (think of me as your visual aid here) are pitifully slow learners, the topic is perfectly relevant.

So let me ask you this. Have you ever been in love? I mean, really in love. You know, stars in your eyes, fireworks, heart palpitations, the whole bit. The kind where, first, you lose your heart, and then—you guessed it—your mind checks out too.

That's what happens, I guarantee you. If you

don't believe me, look deeply into the eyes of a lovesick teenager. See anybody home? I rest my case.

So it follows that people in love do stupid things. Not just silly things, though they do those too. Stupid! In fact, that's how you know that your mind, as well as your heart, has been lost, at least temporarily. Your decisions are no longer made by your brain cells. They are now being dictated by hormones.

The dictionary defines hormones as—are you ready for this?—"a product of living cells that circulates in body fluids and has a specific effect on some other cells."

Give me a break. Do we all know what those "other cells" are? I just told you, right? Brain cells. No doubt about it. When the hormones take over, the brain cells are out to lunch.

Wait a minute, you say. That might be true of teenagers, but adults know better. Oh, yeah?

Ever ask the police why it's so hard to successfully prosecute domestic violence cases? Because the same battered, bruised, bloody woman who one night calls them for help later decides to give the guy "another chance." Why? Because she "loves him." Make sense to you?

In all fairness though, men can get bitten by the "love bug" just as often—and as severely—as women. Take Matthew, for instance. Matthew was my best friend's little brother and lived directly next door to me. He was what was commonly known as the "neighborhood pest."

Throughout his growing-up years, Matthew viewed women as "the enemy." He had nothing but disdain for those of the male sex who fell prey to women's charms.

"I will never get married!" he declared, time and time again. Then, to cover all his bases, he'd add, "But if I ever do, it won't be a big wedding. And for sure I'm not having any kids!"

I'll never forget when he met Sarah. She was working as a grocery checker, and Matthew had stopped in on his way home from work for a loaf of bread. Before the evening was over, he had bought an entire week's worth of groceries—one item at a time! And, no matter how many other checkers were available to wait on him, he stood patiently in line at Sarah's checkstand.

Well, suffice it to say, it was the biggest wedding our neighborhood had ever seen. And when I went to visit Matthew and Sarah soon after their son, Jason, was born, I was more than slightly amused to find the I'll-never-have-any-kids neighborhood pest sitting in the middle of the floor, calmly changing the baby's diaper.

"Hey, Kathi," he asked, as I sat down on the couch next to him, "could you please pass me the wipey-dipeys?"

No comment. Except to say that, sooner or later, it happens to the best of us — as hindsight will verify. As I have progressed through my teens, twenties, thirties, and . . . well, let's not get into that. The point is, whatever your age, some things seem to be unchangeable — especially when it comes to love. I have seen people:

- overjoyed by love;
- destroyed by love;
- completed by love;
- and defeated by love.

But one thing you can count on. Everyone is

changed by love. It may be for the better, it may not. But always, there is a change.

Why? Because as soon as you say, "I love you," it won't be long until some sort of action on your part will be required to prove those words.

"If you love me, you'll...."

"If you really loved me, you'd...."

Fill in the blanks. I'm sure you can. We all have at some time or another. But it's scary, isn't it? Because to act on your declaration of love leaves you vulnerable. At the mercy of a fallible, and often fickle, human being. What else but love could cause us to act so irrationally?

But I don't have to worry about those things anymore. Not because I'm too old for romance (contrary to popular opinion), but because I have finally, really, truly, once-and-forever, fallen IN LOVE!

I mean it. He's the most wonderful, the sweetest, the kindest, the gentlest, the most thoughtful—as a matter of fact, He's perfect. And you know what? He loves me so much, He died for me.

Actually, this love relationship all began way

back on July 5, 1974—the day I first met Jesus face-to-face. And you know what? I fell so deeply in love with Him that day that I immediately pledged to do anything He wanted me to do—for the rest of my life—so long as it did not include public speaking.

You see, one of the reasons I enjoy writing so much is that it gives me a chance to express myself without having to stand up in front of a group of people and risk making a fool of myself. So I thought my writing ministry was "safe" because I could do it in the privacy of my own office. What I didn't know was that once you start publishing books on a regular basis, people expect you to leave your safe little office and go out into the world and talk about those books.

"This is a joke, right, Lord? You don't really expect me to do this, do You? I mean, remember the part about no public speaking? Anything else, Lord, but not this!"

If you love Me...

"But, Lord, I can't!"

If you love Me...

"But I'm scared!"

If you love Me...

"But what if I fail?"

Then He wrapped His arms around me and whispered to my heart the most profound truth I have ever learned.

"All you ever need to know about love," He said, "is that love never fails" (1 Cor. 13:8).

My eyes grew wide. "Never, Lord?" I asked.

"Never," He assured me.

My heart longed to believe Him, but my mind was already busy replaying the many times throughout my life when I had shed countless tears in the name of love. If love never fails, why had my heart been shattered so many times?

"What about the time...?" I began.

"That wasn't love," He explained. "That was need. Love gives, need takes. That's why it failed."

I nodded. He was right. But what about that other time, when...? Before I could speak, He answered.

"That wasn't love either," He said. "It was lust. Lust is another taker, like need. They are often found together, masquerading as love, deceiving many. Then, when they have left their victims bruised and battered, love gets the blame. The real tragedy is that love has been waiting there all the time, longing to heal the brokenhearted, yet so few ever hear or respond to love's voice."

Love's voice. Tears filled my eyes as I realized that right then, at that very moment, I was listening to love's voice. And I resolved that I would not be one of those who did not respond.

"Yes, Lord," I said. "I have heard Your voice and I believe You. It may have taken me a lot of years to understand about love, but now I know. Love never fails."

EXCUSE ME, MA'AM...

"PAPER OR PLASTIC, MA'AM? Ma'am? Excuse me, ma'am?"

Do you know what a shock it is the first time you realize that the bag boy (or is that bag person? I'm almost sure it's not bag lady) at the grocery store is addressing you as "ma'am"? I mean, it doesn't seem like that long ago when my mother was teaching me to respect my elders—and now I am one!

It's a strange feeling, isn't it? True, the term "ma'am" is meant to convey respect, but it's hard to keep that in mind when hearing it makes you feel like Methuselah.

But I have a theory. It isn't that I'm as old as the people I used to refer to as "ma'am" and "sir"; it's that people are being born at a younger age.

Think about it. When was the last time you checked out the age of a fireman or a policeman or an ambulance driver? Surely they don't allow them to participate in these professions before the age of fourteen, and yet none of the ones I've seen lately looked old enough to shave.

I used to laugh at my mother-in-law's story of "that young whippersnapper of a policeman, still wet behind the ears," who had pulled her over for driving too slowly.

"Why, I told him I didn't need any advice from him," she explained. "After all, I was driving before he was born."

He must have been impressed with her logic, because he let her go with only a warning—which she ignored completely.

But now I'm beginning to think maybe she was right. I mean, they're graduating those guys from the police academy younger and younger all the time. (I wonder if that's why some of them ride bikes instead of driving cars—they're simply not old enough to get a driver's license.)

The worst thing, however, is when you go to the doctor and he looks like he just blew in from an after-school sock hop. (OK, so I'm exaggerating. But braces on a surgeon do not inspire confidence. And when he has to call his mother before he can schedule an operation, I'm outta there!)

Let's face it. We baby boomers are middle-aged people living in a youth-oriented world. And if we're not careful, we'll get sucked right into their mind-set. And if we do that, we'll waste the best years of our lives reminiscing about the "good old days."

Be truthful. What was so good about being young? Would you really want to be a teenager again? (I'd rather eat cat food.) Besides, it only takes about ten years to get used to how old you are, so be patient.

After all, old age is not the end — it's the beginning! The beginning of a time when there will be no more sorrow or grief, no pain or sickness, no wrinkles or cellulite, no more loneliness or death.

Instead, there will be Jesus. Forever.

Personally, I'm inclined to agree with the English poet Robert Browning, who penned these famous lines:

Grow old along with me! The best is yet to be
The last of life, for which the first was made;
Our times are in His hands.*

With that to look forward to, I don't mind a bit
being called "ma'am." In fact, I think I kind of
like it!

---

*Robert Browning, "Rabbi ben Ezra," 1864, Public domain.

MEMORY LANE
REVISITED

THE ONLY THING that makes you feel older than talking to an actual grown-up type person who wasn't even born when you graduated from high school, is to get out your yearbooks and let your kids look through them.

"You've gotta be kidding! That's you?" followed by melodramatic rolling on the floor and endless gales of laughter. Not an endearing reaction.

But you can't blame them. I mean, my junior high yearbooks are full of pictures of guys with greasy ducktails and girls with teased bubbles on their heads, closely resembling motorcycle helmets. So what do you expect? That in itself is embarrassing enough to make you burn your yearbooks in effigy.

And then there's the clothes. My husband is a few years older than I, so he remembers girls wearing poodle skirts and saddle oxfords. I, on the other hand, was part of that infamous "Sixties Generation," so styles had changed drastically between my junior and senior high school years. In fact, by the time I was in high school, our styles were fast becoming so hideous as to conjure up a bad drug trip every time we put them on—even though most of us never touched the stuff.

It's amazing how that era seems to be visiting us once again though. "Peace" and "love," sixties-style, is making a comeback. I've actually seen tie-dyed jeans and headbands and ostrich-shell necklaces for sale by the dozens. And kids, reminiscent of twenty-five years ago, are flashing the peace sign, practicing free love, and getting stoned every chance they get.

Sad. When I graduated from high school in 1966, those were not the legacies I would have chosen to pass on to the next generation. And yet I see it all around me. That same emptiness, that same sense of futility, that same look of despair and hopelessness, all masquerading behind an eerily transparent mask of too-loud laughter and too-forced bravado.

Still, it's understandable that one lost generation would adopt the visible symbols of the preceding lost generation. For you see, no matter our age, we are all searching for the same thing. Whether our search leads us to drugs or alcohol, broken relationships, prison terms, gang membership, or the vice-presidency of a bank, we are still searching for the same thing. And that same thing was the theme of my generation, even as it is today: peace and love.

Everyone wants—and needs—peace and love in their lives. And everyone spends his or her entire life trying to attain them. But only those who turn to the One who is Himself the very embodiment of both peace and love will ever find either.

Guess I'll have to remember that when my grandchildren start asking to look through my old yearbooks. Something tells me, if I can just wait patiently through their floor-rolling and hysterical laughter, I can turn the next stroll down memory lane into an opportunity to introduce them to the One who will fulfill their longing for peace and love—forever.

MICROWAVE MANIA

BEING A CREATURE OF HABIT who does not adapt well to change, I resisted getting a microwave almost as much as I resisted getting my computer. Now I can't imagine how I ever lived without them!

Before I got the microwave, however, all I could think of was how much I was going to miss by having it. You know, the delicious aroma of roast turkey or beef permeating the house (I didn't realize I would also miss out on spending the entire day in a 96 degree kitchen); baking dozens and dozens of yummy Christmas cookies (I hadn't yet discovered the joy of popping a tray of preshaped cookie batter into the microwave for six minutes); or tackling a real homemade apple pie (that was before I discovered those microwave-ready pies in the frozen food section—which, by the way, taste better than mine anyway).

But I will admit this—once I finally gave in and decided to join the electronic age via my Sharp Carousel, I was spoiled in no time. Now I'm incensed if I have to cook anything that takes more than seven-and-a-half minutes, tops!

And you know what? If it's true that stores cater to their customers, then I'm not the only one who feels that way. The frozen food section of my grocery store has been taken over by microwave-ready foods—frozen dinners, desserts, breakfasts, pastries, vegetables—even chocolate shakes!

But it makes sense. After all, we live in a world governed by a microwave mania mind-set: i.e., I want it, and I want it right now—if not sooner! Patience is no longer considered a virtue or an asset, but rather a liability that holds people back from becoming "all they can be"—which means, whatever they can run over the top of somebody else to get.

No, we just don't have time anymore to spend the day making a special dinner for our loved ones

or just goofing off at the park with our children—
or grandchildren, as the case may be. We've got
people to see, things to do, places to go. Just like
the rabbit in *Alice in Wonderland,* our theme song
has become, "I'm late, I'm late, for a very important date!" Although we may be right, if the truth
be known, most people who are in such a hurry
have no idea just what it is they're late for or
where it is they're rushing to.

The ironic thing about all this is, these same
people who spend their time rushing blindly from
one meeting and/or appointment to another are
the same people who try to slow—or preferably
stop—the aging process through whatever outra-
geously expensive beauty treatments they can find.
(How else could people still be making money off
of Marvelous Myrtle's Miracle Mudpacks, guaran-
teed to evaporate wrinkles in three easy applica-
tions; or Winnie's Weight-loss Wonder Pills,
promised to melt off pounds while you sleep?)

The very thing they are trying to ignore by staying so busy and covering up with more and more
makeup—their mortality—is the same thing they
are rushing toward at breakneck speed. It stares

back at them every morning when they get up and look in the mirror. A date everyone has to keep sooner or later. A date that Hebrews 2:15 describes as characterized by a "fear of death" that grips people throughout "all their lifetime" and holds them "subject to bondage." However, verse 14 comforts us with the knowledge that Jesus, through His substitutionary death for us, destroyed "him who *had* the power of death, that is, the devil" (italics mine), and released us from that fear.

For those of us who have received Christ's substitutionary death as our own, we have already kept our appointment or date with death. Unlike Alice's rabbit, we are not late for a very important date—we're early! We died almost 2,000 years ago at Calvary!

So what are we rushing around for, caught up in "microwave mania" like the ones who have not yet had their date with death? If we're in a hurry, it should be for only one reason—to proclaim the Gospel to every corner of the earth so that Jesus can come back and take us home!

Even so, come *quickly,* Lord Jesus!

DON'T LOOK NOW BUT...
I THINK I'VE TURNED
INTO MY MOTHER

BEFORE I SAY ANOTHER WORD, I think I had better clarify right up front that I love my mother very much. We are extremely close and, in fact, get along much better now than we did when I was a child (particularly as a teenager). But I have to say that I believe the reason for this is because I understand her so much better now—as a matter of fact, I am fast becoming her clone!

You know what I mean. All those things she used to say and do that I thought were so weird and chalked up to being "old," suddenly I catch myself saying and doing the exact same things. Worse than that, they seem normal. Scary.

For instance, I remember when Christmas was still four days away and I thought it would *never* get here because, after all, four days was a really long time back then. My mother would be in a frenzy at that point, rushing around trying to clean the house, decorate the tree, wrap packages, and bake 893 hand-decorated cookies. I quickly learned not to hang around her much during that time because she would always put me to work and then rush off mumbling, "I can't believe Christmas is here again! I wish it were still a month away."

Now, even with pre-Christmas sale catalogs coming out in July, I too go rushing around four days before Christmas, wishing that I could just go to sleep until January 2—and all I have to do is run down to the bakery to pick up my hand-decorated cookies! (Which just goes to prove, times may have changed, but the passing of it still accelerates with age.)

Another thing I could never understand was why my mom looked forward to a "quiet evening at home" more than a day at Disneyland. I mean, does that make any sense? Well, it does if you've ever spent eighteen hours standing in line with three screaming kids, waiting behind 250 people to get on another gut-wrenching ride and wondering who would throw up first. Besides, a quiet evening at home doesn't set you back a month's salary.

But kids haven't yet learned any of this important stuff. They're still concerned with "having fun" above all else. Why, I can remember being able to jump into a swimming pool without having to worry about redoing my hair and makeup! All that time I was growing up, splashing in the pool and watching my mother sitting in the shade drinking iced tea, I thought she just didn't own a bathing suit. (Now I know better. She had one, just like I do. But the older you get, the fewer people there will be who will ever see you in it!)

In spite of all that, however, I can say this honestly—I can't think of anyone I'd rather "turn into" than my mother. She is a lady who serves and loves the Lord with all her heart and who prayed me into the kingdom. And so, whether I'm rushing around preparing for the holidays, longing for a quiet evening at home, or sitting in the shade drinking iced tea beside the pool, I gladly try to model myself after my mother, loving and serving the Lord with all my heart and praying faithfully for my family.

I intend to pass this on to my children.

WHAT'S IN A NAME?

I WASN'T A BIG SPORTS FAN during my teens or twenties, but there are some names that, whether you followed sports or not, you just knew. Rosey Grier was one of them.

I mean, even if you didn't know him as part of the "Fearsome Foursome," you at least knew he was involved in the capture of the late Senator Robert Kennedy's assassin, Sirhan Sirhan, or that he enjoyed doing needlepoint.

And so, when one of the publishers I work with called me and asked if I would be willing to meet with Rosey Grier to discuss the possibilities of working on a book together, I jumped at the chance. And I just knew my eat-sleep-and-breathe-sports sons would be impressed.

I called my oldest son first. Al was in his early twenties then and followed football religiously.

"You'll never guess who I'm having lunch with next Friday," I said when he answered the phone.

"Who?" he asked.

"Rosey Grier," I answered.

Silence. Then, "That's nice. Who's she?"

I couldn't decide whether to go through the phone and throttle him, or call the nearest rest home and make my reservation. Good grief, my own mother, who never sat through an entire football game in her life, knew immediately who Rosey Grier was. And here was my son, who hadn't missed a game since he was old enough to turn on the TV, and he didn't even know Rosey Grier was of the male gender!

There's only one explanation. Rosey (forgive me if you're reading this, my friend) is too old. I mean, he simply is no longer a household name. The younger generation has never even heard of him!

Of course, Rosey's not the only one. Most young people have never heard of Groucho Marx or Calvin Coolidge, either, so I suppose Rosey's in good company. But the recognition of once-famous names sure separates the lambs from the old goats, doesn't it?

And yet, I suppose I shouldn't be too upset. After all, our children's futures don't hinge on whether or not they recognize names like Ginger Rogers and Fred Astaire. And the fact that they don't doesn't necessarily imply that we have been remiss as parents in teaching them about these people.

But there is one name — the name that is above all names — that we must teach our children. That name is Jesus. Acts 4:12 declares, "Nor is there salvation in any other, for there is no other name under heaven given among men by which we must be saved." When it's all said and done, it makes no difference at all what names our children do or do not recognize — except the name of Jesus. Because that is the name upon which their entire future — indeed their entire eternity — rests.

Let's don't worry too much about whether or not they know Johnny Carson or Johnny Appleseed or even Johnny Unitas. But let's make sure that we introduce them to Jesus, and that they come to know Him intimately. For then we will have performed our jobs as parents honorably.

PARENTING: THE GUILT THAT KEEPS ON GROWING

AS A LITTLE GIRL, I used to make inane comments like, "When I grow up I'm going to have nine kids!" My mother would just look at me, horrified, and say things like, "Well, if you do, it'll serve you right."

Even after becoming a teenager, I still thought a large family would be wonderful. Each time I baby-sat, I pretended that they were my children. I would feed them and play with them and sing to them—and then I'd put them to bed and watch TV until their parents got home.

Nothing to it, right? I just couldn't imagine why people thought it was so difficult. Why, I knew exactly how I would raise my own children once they arrived—how I would discipline them, what I would teach them, what I would allow them to do or not to do. (Doesn't everyone who doesn't have children?)

And then I got married. By the time I had two little ones in diapers, all my preconceived notions of child-rearing had long since gone. This was reality here — life in the trenches. Dr. Spock didn't have a chance.

One thing I noticed during my children's younger years was that, as they grew, so did my sense of guilt. I knew I wasn't coming anywhere close to being a perfect parent and raising perfect children in a perfect family the way I had originally envisioned. And no matter how many times I told myself perfection was an impossible goal, I still felt guilty for not achieving it.

However, in spite of bumbling attempts, quite a few failures, and an ongoing guilt trip, my children managed to grow up. Not without problems, however.

Trust me when I tell you that there is no devastation in life that can begin to compare with the realization that one of your children has a problem — a very serious problem. Particularly if that problem involves something illegal or immoral.

I can remember literally lying on my face before God, weeping, and wondering how this situation could possibly have come into our home. Was it something I did? Something I didn't do? I simply couldn't conceive of the fact that one of my children could be in any sort of trouble except through some fault or negligence on my part.

And then God spoke. He said, "Where you have failed as a parent, confess it. I will forgive and restore. But don't hang on to the guilt, or it will overcome and incapacitate you. Most of all, remember this: I am the only perfect Parent, and I have many wayward children."

That's the key to good parenting, you know. With all our hearts, we are to love them and raise them to God's glory. When we fail, we are to confess it and receive forgiveness and believe God to restore what our failures have taken from our families. But we also have to remember that only God is perfect, and if He has wayward children, then even our own can go astray at times.

But when they do go astray, that is when we must stand firm on God's many promises to bring our wandering offspring home. As He says in Jeremiah 31:16-17: " 'Refrain your voice from weeping, and your eyes from tears; for your work shall be rewarded,' says the Lord, 'and they shall come back from the land of the enemy. There is hope in your future,' says the Lord, 'that your children shall come back to their own border.' "

The important thing is to keep serving and loving and obeying God, for that is the work that He will reward. And surely the day will come when our children will rise up and call us blessed (see Prov. 31:28).

ANOTHER REUNION?

HOW MANY HIGH SCHOOL or college re-unions have you been to? If it's more than one, you're a slow learner, aren't you? I mean, you actually went back a second time, thinking maybe, *just maybe,* it would be better than the first. (Now, if you've been to three or more, I can only assume that you are a professional masochist by trade.)

Because I moved away from the area right after high school, I missed my five-year reunion but, unfortunately, was able to make it for the tenth. The first thing I learned about reunions is that you have to start preparing for them months ahead. You know what I mean—facials, manicures, shop-ping for just the right dress, deciding how to have your hair done and, most of all, going on a starvation diet to knock off those extra 10 pounds you've been lugging around since you had your last child. (That's for us women, of course; men just shave and put on a clean shirt.)

Then, once you arrive at the reunion, it is crucial to obtain a score card—you know, one that lists who is dating and/or married to whom so you don't commit an inexcusable social gaffe. It is also vitally important to wear your name tag—the one with your high school graduation picture on it. Without a picture ID, you will find yourself being referred to as, "Oh, uh, hi, uh, uh . . . " It's really degrading to have to reintroduce yourself to someone who, during the last dance at the junior prom, promised to love you for eternity and now has no idea who you are.

And if you think going to a reunion will give you a chance to catch up with old friends, forget it. An unwritten rule of reunions is that the "oldies but goodies" music has to be played at such a level that absolutely no one can hear what anyone else is saying. If, however, you are proficient at lip-reading, you may have a chance.

The other fact I have learned about reunions is

that the only place you are less likely to have a good time than at your own reunion is at your spouse's. My husband attended a much smaller high school than I did; therefore, he knew absolutely everyone — especially the female members of the class. Suddenly my husband, the one who would rather have a root canal than attend any sort of social function, turns into the life of the party. As I sit on the sidelines, watching my very own Buddy Holly clone dance the night away, I wonder what happened to the guy who told me he had always hated dances and couldn't imagine why anyone would want to attend one.

Personally, I think I'll pass on any more reunions — mine or his. At least, until the Big One — the one where Jesus meets us all — everyone who is a born-again, blood-washed believer — in the air, and then we get to stay with Him forever! But the thing we need to remember is that even that reunion requires preparation.

Oh, we don't have to worry about a crash diet or having our nails and hair done. But there are some things that need to be taken care of. First and most important, we need to make sure we have responded to the request for an RSVP. See, the invitation has been extended to everyone, but unless we accept the invitation, we can't attend the reunion. And what an event we would miss — dancing angels, praising saints, a banquet full of delicious (and completely nonfattening) delicacies, and most important of all, a chance to see (and become like) the Guest of Honor.

No, it's a reunion I wouldn't miss for the world — literally. Because that's the choice. We can say no to the invitation and hang on to what the world has to offer, or we can let go of this broken and dying world and say yes to Jesus.

I'm going. How about you?

I LEFT MY HEART IN SAN FRANCISCO...BUT MY HUSBAND WANTS TO GO TO BUTTE, MONTANA

VACATIONS KEEP TURNING UP — a bit like bad pennies. And, ever-optimistic beings that we are, we keep looking forward to them, despite the fact that years of experience should have taught us by now that vacations just aren't all they're cracked up to be.

Take my husband, for instance. (I don't mean that literally, in spite of our ongoing vacation controversy.) Larry can't imagine anything more exciting than spending eighteen consecutive days touring cowboy museums. I'm bored to tears in eighteen minutes. And driving across hundreds of miles of flat country where the most exciting thing around is tumbleweed leaves a lot to be desired in my book of vacation thrills.

I guess I thought things would get better when there were no longer any little ones in the backseat, fighting over whose turn it was to sit by the window, threatening to throw up if we went around one more windy road, and refusing to synchronize their bathroom and snack stops.

Once again, the passing of time proved me wrong. True, we no longer have to plan our vacations around school breaks and peak operating hours at Disneyland, but my lifelong dream of spending two weeks lounging in the sun in Tahiti is no closer to being a reality now than it was when disposable diapers filled up two-thirds of all my luggage.

"Tahiti?" my husband asks, blinking his eyes in amazement. "Why would you want to go to Tahiti? It's hot there."

Of course, we all know how cool and comfortable it is touring the Badlands of New Mexico in July, right? However, being much more mature (and spiritual) than I was in my younger days, I have learned to restrain myself from making such obvious comments. Instead, I suggest a workable compromise.

"How about San Francisco?" I ask. "It certainly can't be too hot for you there, and you know how I love to tour all those shops and restaurants."

The glazed look in his eyes tells me I've lost him already, and I may as well get my cowboy boots out, because we're heading for two fun-filled weeks in Butte, Montana.

To tell you the truth though, it's really not that bad. Because my husband is also my best friend, we always have a good time driving to our destination (as long as the air conditioner doesn't give out). And besides, I don't have to cook. That in itself is worth trudging through museums looking at dead things that should long since have been buried.

And, in all fairness to him, he has finally accepted the fact that, to me, "roughing it" means staying in a motel with no room service. Tents and trailers are anathema, as are the proverbial joys of cooking over an open fire and sleeping in close proximity to grizzly bears.

So, all in all, vacations really aren't all that bad — especially when you keep in mind that they're temporary. When we've finally used up the last of five rolls of film taking pictures of dilapidated barns and sagging fence posts, I get excited because I know we're going home. ("Like a horse heading for the barn," explains my husband, alias Cowboy Bob.)

But it's true. No matter how hectic things get during the year, no matter how much you look forward to and long to "get away from it all," isn't it nice to come home again? And isn't that how God intended it to be?

Because going home is what it's all about. I get excited about that, especially when I realize that, the older I get, the closer I am to finally going home — home to be with my heavenly family, where throughout eternity I will never again have to tour another museum. In fact, never again will I even consider taking another vacation, because where could I go that would be better than my eternal home?

Now that's something worth looking forward to!

ALL SHOOK UP!

YES, ONCE AGAIN, I'M ALL SHOOK UP—
and it has nothing to do with being in love. It has
to do with living in Southern California, alias
"Earthquake Country."

Being a native Californian, I must admit I've put
in a lot of years in this state, so it takes a pretty
major earthquake to even get my attention anymore. Those minor sways and rolls go basically
unnoticed. This last Sunday morning, however, we
had a couple of them that were definitely more
than sways and rolls!

But you know what? The first one, which oc-
curred at approximately 5 A.M. and measured 7.4
on the Richter scale, I slept right through! Seriously. While other people were falling out of bed

and scrambling to get under tables and desks, I was oblivious to the whole thing. My poor husband was running around checking for gas leaks and securing heavy furniture and appliances for any aftershocks, and I was still snoozing!

By the time the second quake hit at about 8 A.M., I was up and making breakfast. My biggest concern at that point was that the electricity stay on — not because I cared about being able to finish cooking breakfast, but how would I do my hair if I couldn't plug in my curling iron? (By the time you reach my age, priorities have shifted, right along with weight. I would rather be boiled in oil than have to go running out of my house and risk having someone see me before I've had time to "put my face on." And if you don't know what I'm talking about, you're too young to be reading this book.)

To be honest though, my lack of reaction to earthquakes doesn't have so much to do with the fact that I'm cool under fire — it's simply that familiarity breeds contempt. Anyone who grows up in Southern California learns early on how to maintain his or her equilibrium while the earth is shifting underfoot.

Not so for non-Californians. I am often asked by out-of-staters how I can live in a place that is apt to start rocking and rolling at any given moment. And yet, these same people live in parts of the country that are constantly on hurricane or tornado watch. Now that's scary!

Actually, I haven't lived my entire life right here in Southern California. Although I was born and raised here, I left home at the ripe old age of eighteen, wanting to "experience life." Right.

Well, after trying out various other parts of the country for several years, I migrated back here in my early thirties, ready to accept the fact that I'm a Californian at heart. (Actually, I just found out I'm a wimp who can't stand living anywhere that has an average year-round temperature of less than 75 degrees.)

One of the places I lived during my out-of-state sojourn was in a little town called La Center, located in southwestern Washington, about twenty-five air miles from Mt. Saint Helens. In fact, I could stand out in my front yard and see that snow-capped mountaintop rising majestically into the sky. On the morning of May 18, 1980, I stood, awestruck, and watched that same mountaintop blow up, spewing ash and gas into the air as trees, vegetation, animals—and even people—died. The sight of that black cauldron of smoke and ash boiling some eleven miles into the sky, lightning flashing in and around it, was the most awesome sight I have ever witnessed.

Shortly after the eruption of Mt. Saint Helens, I saw a poster showing the mountain erupting. Underneath it read, "Now that I have your attention. . . . " But T-shirts and posters could just as easily be printed up with the same saying, showing pictures of the aftereffects of an earthquake, the devastation of a hurricane or tornado or forest fire.

You see, it doesn't matter where we live. Natural disasters can—and do—strike anyone, anywhere. We can build emergency shelters, move from one area to another, or try our best to outrun and avoid these calamities. But sooner or later, we have to face the fact that there really is only one place of safety—and that's in "the secret place of the Most High" (see Ps. 91:1). Verses 9 and 10 of that same psalm go on to tell us that if we make the Lord our refuge, even the Most High our habitation, then "no evil shall befall" us. But if we fail to make the Lord our refuge and our habitation, then we're on our own when evil tries to overtake us—whether it comes in the form of an earthquake or fire, sickness or death, poverty or misfortune.

When I left California at the age of eighteen, I had not yet made the Lord my refuge or habitation. In fact, I seldom gave Him more than a passing thought. But by the time I came back, I had learned that there is no other Savior, no other Lord, no other Rock. I had also learned that, no matter how old I get, when I am standing on that Rock, I can never be shaken.

Not even when I live in "Earthquake Country."

TIMBER!

I CANNOT TELL YOU the number of times I have dreamed that I was a lumberjack, cutting down trees with a buzz saw, and yelling "Timber!" as they come crashing down — only to wake up and realize it was my husband, Larry, sleeping on his back again and snoring like a freight train.

After all these years, you'd think I'd be used to it. But I still haven't gotten over that first night we were married, when I woke up, terrified, and called the police to report that an airplane was repeatedly buzzing our home. Imagine my dismay to learn that we were not being attacked by a crazed Red Baron, but instead that horrible noise was coming from my dearly beloved, the one I had just promised to sleep next to " 'til death us do part."

And yes, I'll admit it, that phrase echoed through my mind night after sleepless night, causing me to entertain some less-than-loving (and quite a bit less-than-Christlike) thoughts. Oh, I've tried rolling him back over on his side, but once asleep, he's a dead weight. So I poke him—repeatedly—until I wake him up.

"Huh? What?" he asks, interrupting his nightly sonata for a few blessed moments.

"Sorry to wake you, but you're snoring," I whisper. "Please turn over."

"Huh? What?"

"Snoring," I repeat. "Turn over!"

"Huh? What?"

"Over!" I yell. "Turn over *now!*"

Still mumbling "huh" and "what," he rolls over, not so much because he finally understood what I said, but because he wants to get away from me so he can go back to sleep.

By that time, of course, I'm wide awake, and the harder I try to get back to sleep before he rolls over onto his back once again, the more sure I am that I'm destined to spend the rest of my nights lying in bed, staring into the darkness, reminding myself that a pillow over his head is not an option.

And then I met Verna. Now Verna is somewhat older than I and has been married quite a bit longer, and therefore, I respect her wisdom. So when she told me about earplugs and how they had saved her marriage (and her husband's life), I decided to give them a try.

It was wonderful! I couldn't hear a thing. And I actually slept through the night without having to stumble into the living room in desperation and sleep on the couch.

Life was good once again. Larry could snore to his heart's content, I could sleep, and there was hope that we might even live to see our fiftieth wedding anniversary. But there was one catch.

You see, when I put my earplugs in, not only do I drown out the sound of Larry's snoring, I drown out all other sounds as well. If the phone rings during the night to tell me someone I love has just been taken to the hospital emergency room, I don't hear it. If the smoke alarm goes off to alert me to the fact that my home is burning down around me, I don't hear it. If my teenage son forgets his key and comes home after I've gone to bed and starts ringing the bell and pounding on the door, I don't hear it.

True, I can count on my husband to alert me to these noises — should he miraculously be able to hear them above his own snoring — but it makes me uneasy to think that I can't hear these important sounds for myself. Although, at certain times and under certain circumstances, it's OK to depend on others to convey to us certain facts that we cannot ascertain for ourselves, there are other times that we must perceive things on our own.

The reality of God's love, for instance. Although pastors and Sunday School teachers and parents and friends can tell us about the love of God and of His great gift to us in the person of His dear Son, Jesus Christ, none of that will be real to us until we experience it for ourselves. And then, once we have personally experienced God's love, we must cultivate that love-relationship on an ongoing, personal basis. "Hanging out" with other Christians, although that is a wise thing to do, will not, in and of itself, make us more like Christ. "Hanging out" with Jesus and listening to and obeying His Word will.

And that's why, however helpful my foam rubber earplugs have been for me, I don't ever want to be guilty of wearing spiritual earplugs. Sound silly? Not really. Think about the last time you lay awake listening to your husband snore beside you. Grated on your nerves, didn't it? Irritated you, didn't it? You bet it did! Well then, what about the last time you lay awake, listening to the Holy Spirit convict you of something in your life that needed to be corrected? Made you very uncomfortable, didn't it? Made you want to get some spiritual earplugs to drown out the noise and get back to sleep. Right?

But the voice of the Holy Spirit is nothing like your husband's snores. God's voice cannot be ignored or drowned out — not without dire consequences, that is. Because of that, I have asked the Lord to give me "ears to hear" (Matt. 11:15) whatever He would speak to me — and a heart to obey whatever I hear Him speak.

And as long as I am hearing and obeying whatever He speaks to me, His peace will enable me to sleep — no matter what.

Even when lumberjacks are cutting down trees and crazed Red Barons are buzzing overhead.

CHANGED YOUR BABY TIRE LATELY?

WHEN I WAS GROWING UP, no one ever dreamed I would someday become an auto mechanic. It's a good thing too because they would have been disappointed.

Oh, I know, times have changed. Girls can aspire to any career that interests them — auto mechanics included. But since I have always hated getting my hands dirty and am not interested in anything that even vaguely resembles a motor, I certainly can't take any credit for blazing the trail for those future female mechanics. And, to be perfectly honest, I can't think of any of the girls I grew up with being interested enough in pistons and intake valves to even make an attempt at getting into the high school auto shop class.

But, as I said, times have changed. The generation immediately following us no longer divides up careers or hobbies or interests as "boy things" and "girl things." In some ways, I suppose that's OK. But for me, even if I had been a part of the younger generation rather than a baby boomer, I still doubt I would have had any interest in spending my spare time underneath a car.

Fortunately, I don't have to. You see, I married a man who loves cars so much he actually names them — and talks to them. It's a bit unnerving, but at least I know where he spends every spare minute of his time. You guessed it — the garage.

And what a garage it is! This same man who has never properly hung up a wet towel in his entire life sees nothing unusual about alphabetizing the tools in his garage. And, although you probably wouldn't want to try eating off my kitchen floor, you should be perfectly safe doing so in Larry's garage. In fact, several years ago when we were in the process of selling our old home and moving into our present one, the realtor seriously considered listing our place as an "immaculate garage with house attached."

Larry keeps his cars in exactly the same condition as his garage — immaculate — washing them every time a piece of dust dares to land on them, threatening any bird that flies overhead, forbidding any and all food consumption in or near the vehicles, and insisting they be parked a minimum of two football fields away from the store to prevent anyone accidentally running into them with a grocery cart.

I don't mind abiding by those rules — most of the time, anyway. But when it comes to learning the mechanical end of car upkeep, I draw the line. That's what I have him for, right? So why should I have to learn those highly technical things, like how to pump your own gas?

I'll never forget the first time I tried to do that. I had seen my husband go around to the back of the car and bend down to pump the gas, so I figured the gas tank had to be back there somewhere. Well, I walked around back there for the longest time — gas hose in hand, by the way — but I couldn't see a thing. I finally gave up and limped home on fumes, only to have my more-than-slightly-amused husband explain to me that the gas tank was underneath the license plate. (What a dumb place to put it!)

So, from then on, I simply refused even to attempt anything mechanical. On occasion, though, circumstances have dictated otherwise.

Like the day I got a flat tire. Now, I had a choice of ignoring the flopping and bumping and pretending I didn't know what was wrong in hopes of driving home so my husband could change the tire (but since that was several miles, even I knew that wasn't a good idea), or stopping and changing the tire myself.

I chose none of the above. I parked and locked the car, then walked home and handed Larry the keys. When I explained to him what had happened, he decided it would be a good idea for me to go with him and watch him change the tire in case this sort of thing ever happened again.

He gave up entirely on that idea though, the minute he pulled the spare tire out of the trunk. Because our car was fairly new, the spare was one of those small tires that will work to get you where you need to go to get it replaced, but is certainly not meant to be used for any length of time.

I, of course, didn't know this, and had never seen such a small spare tire. Consequently, I made a comment that my husband has never let me live down. I said, "Oh, look, a baby tire!"

I'll let you in on a little secret though. While he chuckles and teases me about "baby tires" and my general ignorance of things mechanical, I just smile sweetly and refuse to argue. After all, it worked, didn't it? I mean, he has never again suggested I learn how to change a tire.

To be perfectly honest, I think it's wonderful that young women are becoming more adept at handling these sorts of things. I mean, there's no guarantee there'll be anyone else around the next time you need to change a tire or pump gas or alphabetize your tools.

On the other hand, it probably wouldn't hurt men to learn how to hang up their towels or heat their own TV dinners either. But you know what? Deep down, we all know that we could do for ourselves many of the things our loved ones now do for us. The thing is, why take away the chance for someone to show love in a tangible way? If my husband prefers changing baby tires to changing babies, and if I prefer hanging up wet towels to hanging up tools on their properly coded racks, why rock the boat?

At the same time, if my granddaughter would rather learn how to clean an air filter than the kitchen, I suppose I should encourage her to do just that. To do anything else would definitely not be an act of love. And acts of love, rather than division of duties, are what successful relationships are all about.

And to be even more specific, successful relationships are what life is all about. Whether we end up as an auto mechanic, a lifeguard, a TV show host, or President of the United States, what good is any of it if we don't have satisfying and fulfilling relationships?

Especially with our Creator. The One who breathed life into us and loved us and died for us— the One who is coming back for those of us who have established a love relationship with Him. When wet towels and baby tires and immaculate garages and all those other so-called "boy things" and "girl things" have passed away—and they will—the only thing left will be our relationship with Jesus.

The rest, with or without automotive grease, is just so much fluff.

I DON'T DO WINDOWS

WHEN I WAS A TEENAGER, blackmailed into doing "chores" in order to get my allowance, I naively believed that someday I would outgrow my hatred of housework. (After all, Donna Reed always seemed to enjoy vacuuming her carpets in her high heels, housedress, and apron; and Harriet Nelson never tired of baking cookies for her family, as well as for the rest of the neighborhood.) But I was wrong.

I still hate housework. And I don't do windows—or wash baseboards, or clean closets, or polish silver, or check behind the furniture for cobwebs. Not very often, anyway. Oh, once or twice a year when out-of-town relatives are coming for a visit I do all that stuff—but I still hate it.

If I ever write a best-seller, the first thing I'll do is hire a housecleaner. Not a housekeeper — a housecleaner. You see, I keep my house very neat all the time — I just don't clean it.

What this means is that a burglar will never break into my house some morning after I've gone to work and find unmade beds, unwashed dishes, newspapers scattered across the floor, or unfolded towels in the bathroom. He will not become disgusted at the sight of toothpaste or whiskers in the sink. Nor will he feel nauseous from looking at three-day-old food encrusted on the burners of the stove. (Unless, of course, I have been foolish enough to go out of town and leave my teenager in charge.)

But pity the poor guy if he has any allergies and decides to go rummaging around in the back of one of my dusty closets. And if he tries to escape through a window, I hope he's wearing gloves. The last time I went near my windows with Windex and a squeegee, I got sick and changed my mind. Much easier to just keep the curtains closed.

Which brings me to my point. Could it be that I live my spiritual life the way I clean house? Do I just do "surface cleaning" so I will appear holy and spiritual to others? Am I ignoring all those dirty corners, all those filthy cupboards and closets?

Because if I am, it won't do any good. When Jesus comes for me, He won't call ahead to let me know He's coming. There won't be any time for cleaning then. Everything I've tried to keep hidden will be brought to light. And I'll be so embarrassed.

No, some things we don't outgrow — no matter how old we get. We just have to make a decision to let the Holy Spirit search out all those hidden corners of our hearts, and then resolve to cooperate with Him in an ongoing clean-up project.

Housework isn't fun. Heartwork can be even tougher. But it's worth the price, I promise.

Adapted from *A Moment a Day* by Mary Beckwith and Kathi Mills (Ventura, Calif.: Regal Books, 1988). Used by permission.

I DON'T WANT TO WORRY YOU, BUT...

"I DON'T WANT TO WORRY YOU, but . . . "

Ever hear that statement? Of course you have. Ever start worrying the minute you heard it? Of course you did. Especially if you're a mother.

Don't get me wrong. I don't mean to imply that fathers don't worry; it's just that mothers do it so much better. (Practice makes perfect, right?)

Experience has taught me that, anytime someone starts a sentence with that particular phrase, the rest of the sentence is not good news.

"I don't want to worry you, but . . . what flight number was it that your sister was on?"

"I don't want to worry you, but . . . you know that brush fire behind your house that they said was under control?"

"I don't want to worry you, but . . . didn't you say your son was supposed to be in school today?"

"I don't want to worry you, but . . . you know that snake I brought home for the science project?"

"I don't want to worry you, but . . . you know how you were saying you plan to stay at your job until you retire?"

"I don't want to worry you, but . . . which bank was it you said you kept all your money in?"

You can't have lived as long as I have and not have heard that phrase numerous times. And each time you heard it, that familiar knot started forming in your stomach—followed by shortness of breath and a distant buzzing in your ears. Right?

It was no different the time my husband called me while I was in Los Angeles, attending a work-related seminar. After a few minutes of small talk, he said, "Oh, by the way, I don't want to worry you, but . . . you don't happen to remember when Chris had his last tetanus shot, do you?"

Now, I tried very hard to remain calm, telling myself that he was simply asking this out of curiosity, assuming that I undoubtedly carried the children's shot records with me everywhere I went. I *tried* to tell myself that, but I knew better.

"I'll jump in the car and be home in under two hours," I said. "Which hospital should I meet you at?"

Several hours—and several stitches—later, Chris' head was almost as good as new, and we had all survived another "I don't want to worry you, but . . . " crisis. I have to admit though, my continuing reaction to this phrase was beginning to nag at me.

Sure, I'm a mother. And mothers worry. After all, it's our job, isn't it? Well, actually, no, it isn't.

Although it may be a very normal reaction to start worrying the minute we hear that phrase—particularly if the remainder of the sentence has to do with a loved one—as Christians, we need to be practicing what we preach. After all, we spend a lot of time telling unbelievers that they need to trust Jesus— and yet, when the rubber meets the road, trust goes out the window and worry comes in.

Most of us are familiar with the Scripture in 1 Peter, which tells us to cast "all your care upon Him, for He cares for you" (5:7). But that's a lot easier said than done, isn't it? Especially when it involves our children.

And yet, do we really think we are better parents than our Heavenly Father? Do we actually believe that we love our children more than God does? With our limited abilities, do we somehow imagine that we can offer them better protection than the One who is omniscient, omnipresent, and omnipotent?

One of the Scriptures that has become a mainstay for me as I learn to trust God is Isaiah 49:25, which says, "For I will contend with him who contends with you, and I will save your children." There are a lot of things in this world that contend with us for our children's affections, their time, their love, even their lives and their very souls. But the primary one who contends with us for our children is Satan himself. Now I don't know about you, but I sure don't want to take him on in my own strength. Doesn't it make a lot more sense to allow the One who has promised to contend with him for our children's sakes to do just that? But freeing God to do that for us means trusting Him — even in the face of an "I don't want to worry you, but . . . " crisis.

I know. It isn't easy. But then, what's the alternative? Worrying ourselves into an ulcer or a nervous breakdown isn't going to help anyone. Besides, putting our loved ones in God's faithful hands is one of the smartest things we can ever do.

Remember, the reason we cast all our cares on Him is because He cares for us. On top of that, He never changes, and He never leaves or forsakes us. Walking in that truth will bring us to "the peace of God, which surpasses all understanding" (see Phil. 4:7), even in the face of another "I don't want to worry you, but . . . " crisis.

STAYING ALIVE AT 55

NO, I DO NOT GET DISCOUNTS at Denny's, I am not getting ready to apply for Social Security, nor am I checking out retirement homes—yet. When I say, "Staying Alive at 55," I'm referring to the way I drive.

I call driving at a maximum speed limit of 55 mph safe and sane. My teenage son refers to it as "boring." My husband calls it extremely dangerous.

"How can you drive down the freeway at 55 when everyone else is going at least 60?" he asks. "It's dangerous. It's people like you who cause accidents." (Excuse me, but isn't that a bit like saying, "It's people who work for a living that cause thieves to resort to robbery"?)

I don't mean to be difficult here, but how come I

get criticized for obeying the speed limit? Am I supposed to feel sorry for the guy behind me who's leaning on his horn, trying to incite me to break the law so he can get to wherever he's going on time? I mean, if he has such an important appointment, why didn't he leave earlier? (You know the old saying, "Poor planning on your part does not constitute an emergency on my part"? Well, whoever coined that can have my vote for President.)

To be perfectly honest, however, being known as the only human being on Planet Earth who never exceeds the speed limit or walks on the grass when posted signs tell me not to, and who stops at stop signs out in the middle of nowhere definitely has its downside. Take, for instance, the day I got my one and only speeding ticket.

There I was, driving down a two-lane road with my cruise control set exactly at 50 mph (in accordance with posted speed limits, of course) when a pickup truck passed me like a shot. He barely got back over into the right lane in time to prevent plowing head-on into oncoming traffic.

I'll admit, I was a bit shook up and more than slightly distracted by the incident. So much so, in fact, that I failed to notice the sign announcing a reduced speed zone ahead. I hadn't gone half a mile when I heard a siren and glanced in my rearview mirror to see a red light flashing ominously behind me. I pulled over immediately to allow the police car to pass but, to my surprise, he stopped too.

What in the world could he be stopping me for? I wondered. And then the policeman walked up to my window and presented me with the exact same question.

"Do you know why I pulled you over?" he asked, flipping open his citation book.

"No, I don't," I answered honestly, hoping he was going to ask me to be a star witness against the pickup driver who had zoomed past me earlier.

"You were speeding," he said. "May I see your license and registration, please?"

Having driven for more than twenty years without a ticket, I felt as if I'd just stepped into the Twilight Zone. Surely I was dreaming and would wake up any moment.

Wrong. I had to drive home with a traffic citation sitting on the seat beside me and the officer's parting words ringing in my ears: "If I were you, ma'am, I'd be a lot more careful to drive at or below the speed limit from now on. These signs are posted for your safety, you know."

I could hardly wait to get home and tell my family about my humiliating experience. Surely they would understand how unjust it was for someone like me to receive a speeding ticket. Surely they would smother me with kindness and sympathy.

"You *what?*" cried my husband, when I called him at work to tell him about my ticket. "You got a speeding ticket?" And that was all he said. From then on he was too busy laughing to be able to say anything else.

My son wasn't much better. After wiping the look of shock from his face, he smiled admiringly. "Cool!" was all he said.

Sympathy was not what I received from the traffic school instructor either. Nor did the other participants feel one bit sorry for me. In fact, when I tried to explain to them that this was my very first ticket — ever! — they would just smile knowingly, wink, and nod their heads. "Sure," they would whisper. "I understand. Really! It's my first ticket too." And then they would burst out laughing.

My Heavenly Father, however, reacted quite differently. He didn't laugh at the irony of it all — nor did He commend me by saying, "Cool!" And He certainly didn't mock me and tell me it was His first ticket too.

He just listened. And loved me. And reminded me that He knew exactly what had happened and why I'd gotten the ticket. He also told me that it really didn't matter. That as far as He was concerned, I hadn't ruined my "perfect record." Because in His eyes, I was as perfect as Jesus.

Suddenly I realized that, though it is important to try to obey the law at all times — whether man's law or God's law — none of us has ever done so without failing, at least occasionally. The important thing is, Jesus has already paid the price for all those failures. And when we learn to live within His forgiveness, God looks at us — and sees Jesus.

And so, as I continue down the freeway with my cruise control set at 55 mph, I thank God for sending His Son to assure me of a "perfect record" when I finally pull off at the exit marked "heaven."

ARE THERE WORSE THINGS THAN BEING ALONE?

I ONCE MET a newly divorced woman who carried her ex-husband's photo around in her purse, only to announce to people, "There are worse things than being alone, you know. Would you like to see his picture?" Then, of course, she would laugh all too loudly.

Personally, I thought that was one of the saddest statements I had ever heard, primarily because it was obviously proclaimed out of intense pain. In her attempt to make light of one of life's worst tragedies, she only served to accentuate her loss.

"There are worse things than being alone" is more than a sad statement; it is also a lie. The Bible says, in Genesis 1:31, that "God saw everything that He had made, and indeed it was very good." But then, in Genesis 2:18, He observes, "It is not good that man should be alone."

Oh, I know, in our busy, hectic lives, we look forward to those few and far between times when we can actually be *alone,* if only for a few minutes. Even the most social among us need that occasional respite—particularly if you happen to be a parent with several toddlers and/or teens running in and out all day. I mean, we love them, but . . . well, you know exactly what I mean, right?

And yet I wonder how many of us actually understand why it is that God said, "It is not good that man should be alone." In *Single, Married, Separated & Life After Divorce,* author Myles Munroe declares, "It's OK to be single, but not good to be alone." Sounds good, but what exactly does it mean?

Well, *Strong's Concordance* gives the Hebrew meaning of the word for *alone* as including "separation; a part of the body; apart; only; by self; solitary." Almost makes you sad to read it, doesn't it?

The word *single* is something different. The dictionary defines single as "separate, unique, whole." Now that doesn't sound sad at all. In fact, it sounds like being single is a pretty good thing to be!

Which reminds me of a bumper sticker I've seen many times: "Happiness is being single." Well, if being single means being separate, unique, and whole, then I suppose I'd have to agree that happiness and singleness would definitely go together. However, I'm quite sure the author of that bumper sticker meant to imply that the state of being unmarried is one and the same as the state of happiness. What do you want to bet there are a whole lot of unmarried people who would take exception to that statement!

On the other hand, there are a lot of married people who might think the statement has some merit. The divorce rate in our country is overwhelming, and it grows daily, in part because dissatisfied spouses buy into the illusion that "happiness is being single" — or remarried, or absolutely anything other than the state they are currently living in.

We baby boomers who grew up between the 50s and 70s came of age during an era of incredibly fast-changing and declining morals and standards. In the beginning of that time period, divorce was the exception; by the end of the era, almost everyone had been touched by the devastation of divorce in some way.

Why? Well, one of the main reasons was because we just hadn't figured out the difference between being single and being alone. Most of us rushed off and got married before we had ever become single — i.e., separate, unique, whole — expecting to achieve that wholeness by drawing what was missing in our own lives from our marriage partners. Sadly, our partners were no more single than we were, and therefore, didn't even have enough resources for themselves, let alone any left over to share with us.

And so we self-destructed. We just didn't comprehend the need to be truly single before marrying — and then to remain single afterward! Think about it. Would you want to cease being separate, unique, or whole once you got married? Or would the marriage be a healthier one if viewed as a union between two separate, unique, and whole individuals?

That's why God did not say, "It's not good for man to be single." He had already created Adam as a single individual. Adam was separate, unique, and whole. But God knew he needed another separate, unique, and whole individual to prevent him from being alone. Hence, Eve.

And that's why my friend's statement that "there are worse things than being alone" was so sad—and so untrue. She didn't understand that, of all the things God had created, the only thing He looked upon and declared not good was Adam's aloneness.

We all need each other, not only in a marriage relationship, but in other relationships as well. It is those relationships that prevent us from being alone.

But it is our relationship with God that enables us to be single. Remember, being alone is not good; being single is very good. God desires us to be separate, unique, and whole individuals. But that is a condition we can never achieve apart from Him. A vital, ongoing relationship with the Creator of all life will make us the single individuals we need to be in order to maintain successful relationships with others and avoid the state of being alone.

Because, contrary to what my friend tried so hard to convince herself and others of, there really is nothing worse than being alone.

AT ARM'S LENGTH

SOME OF YOU MAY BE READING this book and wondering whether or not you're old enough to qualify as middle-aged, or even as a baby boomer. Well, look at the book. How far away from your face are you holding it? Assuming you haven't already resorted to reading glasses, and if you're holding the book so far away that you're beginning to wonder what you're going to do when your arms don't stretch any farther, you're old enough.

I guess I didn't notice it so much when my eyes started "aging," since they really hadn't been too great since I was a kid. For me though, it wasn't that I couldn't get things far enough away to read them, it was that I had to get right on top of them to even see them!

So when I was in junior high, my parents "made" me get glasses. No thirteen-year-old wants to be called four-eyes (or worse). I would much rather have walked into walls or stepped out into the street in front of an oncoming bus. Much less painful than being poked fun at by merciless peers.

But I got them anyway. (Of course, I didn't wear them. I'd slide them on before leaving for school in the morning, then slip them back off as soon as I rounded the corner. The only hard part was remembering to put them back on again before I got home.)

Finally, as I got older (and blinder) and maybe even a little smarter, I started wearing my glasses on a regular basis. It was amazing to realize how much I'd been missing by stumbling around in a fog for so many years!

Now I'll admit, I haven't yet gotten to the point where I'm having any serious problems seeing close up, and I'm thankful for that, since I don't relish the idea of adjusting to bifocals. But I remember when my husband, who for years had seemingly perfect vision, suddenly began having trouble reading.

I'd come into the living room and find him leaning back in his favorite chair, trying to hold the
newspaper three feet away while he read. When I
asked him if he thought it was time to have his
eyes checked to see if he needed reading glasses,
he insisted there was absolutely nothing wrong
with his eyes, it was just the newsprint.

Eventually though, he gave in and got the reading glasses. Then he went around telling everyone
how you can tell you've hit middle-age when your
arms are no longer the right length to read by—
ha, ha. I just ignored him, but I have to admit, I
started watching myself very carefully to make
sure I wasn't starting to prop my book up on the
opposite end of the couch when reading.

Maybe, like me, you've worn glasses for years.
Or maybe you're like my husband, just discovering
that your arms are no longer the right length to
read by. Either way, the important thing to
remember is, be thankful for the sight God's given
you to behold His beautiful creation. And above
all, keep your eyes—whatever their age and condition—fixed on Him.

THINK OF
THE STARVING ARMENIANS

THROUGHOUT OUR GROWING-UP YEARS, there are a lot of things that stick with us about our parents, but none more surely than their worn-out bits of nonoriginal parental wisdom. For instance, "The early bird catches the worm"; "A place for everything and everything in its place"; "A stitch in time saves nine"; ad nauseum.

But my very favorite was, "Think of the starving Armenians."

Now I had no idea what an Armenian was, nor did I care. And, to be perfectly honest, when my mother tried to get me to eat my turnips by telling me the starving Armenians would love to have them, there was nothing I wanted more than to wrap those nasty little turnips up and send them to wherever it was the Armenians happened to be. Unfortunately, she would never give me their address.

But I have to admit, more than once I went to bed feeling just terrible that, somewhere in this world, there were people who were actually so hungry they would be glad to have turnips. It boggled my imagination!

And it still does. I didn't raise my own children on stories of starving Armenians, but as I got older (and, hopefully, a bit wiser) I did begin to get an appreciation for what my mother was trying to teach me about being thankful and not wasting the many blessings we so often take for granted.

It's all about being a wise steward. Most of us who have been in the church for any length of time have heard countless teachings on tithing. Some of us accept and obey that teaching; others do not. But even if we practice tithing, do we practice wise use of our resources over and above that tithe?

I believe God holds us accountable to do just that. Jesus said, "For you have the poor with you always" (see Matt. 26:11). We don't have to look very far to verify that truth. (In fact, anyone who's ever financed a teenager through the senior year of high school could serve as a visual aid here.)

Seriously though, with only a few exceptions, most of us have been so blessed that our idea of poverty is not being able to buy a new car every three years. There are so many in our world today (even in our own country) who, like the infamous starving Armenians, really would be thrilled to have our turnips. And, although I firmly believe that our first duty, according to the Great Commission recorded in Mark 16:15, is to "go into all the world and preach the Gospel to every creature," I don't believe our responsibility stops there.

First John 3:17-18 speaks directly to that responsibility: "But whoever has this world's goods, and sees his brother in need, and shuts up his heart from him, how does the love of God abide in him? My little children, let us not love in word or in tongue, but in deed and in truth."

And when we give, we need to be willing to give more than just our turnips. We need to give our best—because that's what God gives us. And, as children of the Heavenly Father, we should model ourselves after Him. I mean, how would we feel if, instead of giving us His best, He just gave us turnips? Why, we'd be a whole lot worse off than the starving Armenians, I guarantee you!

So, the next time you can't sleep, instead of counting sheep, count blessings — and then ask God whom He would have you share them with. And then do it. After all, some of our parents' worn-out bits of nonoriginal parental wisdom had a lot of merit, and "Think about the starving Armenians" is definitely one of them.

MASTERING
BATHROOM ETIQUETTE

THERE ARE FEW THINGS IN LIFE that are simpler to do—and more difficult to figure out why people don't—than changing the toilet paper roll.

I'm serious. Changing toilet paper rolls was something I mastered at an early age—and without a college degree, I might add. And, though I may not have been old enough to do it out of common courtesy, I was certainly old enough to do it out of common sense!

Not so everyone else, I have discovered. However, because toilet paper rolls are a somewhat delicate matter to discuss, I will not identify any of those non-toilet paper roll changers by name.

Instead, let me introduce "Anonymous." Anonymous lives in my house (and probably in yours too). Now, my house has three bathrooms, all of which I endeavor to keep supplied with sufficient toilet paper at all times. However, regardless of which bathroom Anonymous chooses to use at any given time, that is invariably the one where the toilet paper roll comes up empty. Of course, one would think that, after countless years of my nagging — not to mention my numerous offers to give a seminar on the proper care and maintenance of toilet paper rolls — Anonymous would, by now, have gotten the hint and learned to change toilet paper rolls. Not so. In fact, I have come to the conclusion that it has somehow been ordained that only one person per household be designated as the official toilet paper roll changer. (Any guesses who got the dubious honor in our house?)

But let's face it. The world is full of people named "Anonymous," who go through life being decent people of a relatively pleasant sort to live and/or associate with. And yet they have these blind spots — you know what I mean? It makes no difference if they're toddlers or teenagers or baby boomers like us, you can lecture them about these

131

blind spots 'til the cows come home, but they simply will not see what you're talking about.

Like towels, for instance. Everybody knows at least one Anonymous who, for the life of them, simply cannot hang up a towel. Oh, you might train them to throw their sopping wet towel in the general direction of the towel rack—and every now and then, that towel might just catch and hang there—but you will never, ever get them to fold even one single towel and hang it up the way they found it.

It's the same thing with toothpaste tubes. There are some of us who recognize right off that it's just as easy to squeeze a toothpaste tube from the bottom as it is from the middle—and a whole lot more economically sound—but there are others (the infamous group known as "Anonymous Anonymous") who have never even seen the bottom end of a toothpaste tube. They simply squeeze from the middle until the top half is used up and then throw it away and get another one. (Of course, these are the very same people who don't realize that the cap from the top of the toothpaste tube is actually supposed to be screwed back on after every use.)

And so, the official toilet paper roll changer
also has to go in and police the towel and toothpaste departments of the bathroom as well. Now,
for those of you who, like me, have had this dis-
tinction bestowed on you by default, be honest.
Do you find yourself doing this job with a slightly
less than sweet disposition at times? Do you mum-
ble and grumble and moan and groan and com-
plain about how thoughtless and inconsiderate
Anonymous is? If so, let me tell you about Susie.

I hadn't been a Christian for more than a year
or two when I first met Susie. Susie and Jim had
been married about five years but had no children.
Jim, however, was always bringing home "strays"—
someone who'd shown up at the local soup kitchen
hoping for a meal and possibly even a warm bed
for a night or two; a runaway teenager with a drug
problem; even homeless families on occasion.

At this particular time, there were almost ten
people living in their home. It was Thursday afternoon, and Susie had decided to mop the kitchen
floor before Jim came home. She was almost
through when Jim, with two new strangers in tow,
burst through the back door, right onto the freshly

scrubbed linoleum. One look at the footprints they left behind as they crossed the floor toward her told Susie they had obviously taken a shortcut through some muddy river bottom before arriving at her home.

Susie opened her mouth to voice (quite loudly) her objection and irritation over the untimely invasion when she noticed something strange about the footprints of the smaller of the two strangers. Looking closer, she realized that the sole of one of his shoes had obviously worn completely through, and it was actually the bottom of his bare foot that was making part of the mark on her floor.

Suddenly, she remembered Jesus' words in Matthew 25:40: "Inasmuch as you did it to one of the least of these My brethren, you did it to Me." She swallowed her objections, smiled at her guests, and offered them something to eat.

So the next time you get stuck with "bathroom duty," remember Susie. More important, remember the words of Jesus, swallow your objections, smile, and ask the Lord if there is anything else you can do for your very own Anonymous. Because, after all, they (the members of Anonymous

Anonymous) really are decent people of a relatively pleasant sort — and life without them would be a poor trade-off for not having to change the toilet paper roll anymore.

Don't you agree?

YOU CAN'T WATER CAMELS ON BACK-TO-SCHOOL NIGHT

HAVE YOU EVER NOTICED how we humans have this tendency to believe that, just as soon as we manage to work our way through our immediate crises, we'll actually have some spare time on our hands? You know what I mean. "Well, I can't help with children's ministries this month, but next month when I've finished this project I'm working on right now, and when my out-of-town company leaves, and when I finish wallpapering my office, sure, I'll be glad to. Sign me up!" Trouble is, next month rolls around and so do several more crises and projects and possibly even more out-of-town guests, and we end up with no more spare time than we had the month before.

In fact, I used to be so foolish as to think that

once I got "old" (you know, thirty or forty something), I would already have done everything important to do and would therefore have all sorts of
free time. Ha!

Eventually, however, reality slapped me in the
face and I finally learned—out of desperation—
how to cope with ongoing crises and never enough
time to handle them—even though I was beginning to think I'd die of old age trying. So would
you like to know the secret? OK, I'll tell you—it's
laughter. Let me illustrate.

It happened one morning several years ago,
while I was gulping my coffee and clearing the
table, trying not to trip over the cat who was anxiously rubbing against my legs in hopes of being
fed, and reminding Chris, my then ten-year-old
(for the eighth time), to finish his breakfast or
he'd be late for school. That's when the phone
rang. It was an irate mother wanting to know what
I was going to do about getting her little Penelope
transferred out of Miss Ogre's classroom and into
another classroom where the teacher would appre-
ciate Penelope's "sensitive nature."

Balancing the receiver on my shoulder, I managed to catch my son as he raced past me, thrust his lunch into one hand, his jacket into the other, and kissed the air as the door slammed behind him.

I sighed and began washing dishes as Penelope's mother droned on. I hadn't remembered this being listed as one of my duties when I accepted the position of Community and School Association president.

I finally convinced Penelope's mother that she really needed to call the school and make an appointment with the principal and/or Miss Ogre. Then, finished with the breakfast dishes, I decided to listen to one of my favorite radio programs while I made the beds.

I flipped the switch just in time to hear the speaker tell how Abraham had sent his servant to get a wife for his son, Isaac. When the servant arrived at his destination, it was "the time when women go out to draw water" (Gen. 24:11). He went on to explain how Rebekah drew water, not only for Abraham's servant, but for all ten of his camels as well.

As I finished the beds and was separating a

mountain of dirty clothes, I heard him say, "Of course, that was in the days before automatic washers and dryers or microwave ovens. Let me tell you, in those days, women really worked!"

Gasping, I stared at the radio in disbelief. "Oh, yeah?" I hollered, snatching my pile of perma-press from the floor, "well, let me tell you something. . . . "

I was still muttering under my breath when I stormed out of the house fifteen minutes later, heading for my part-time job as church secretary. As I sat at my desk, fingers flying over the type-writer keys in a vain attempt to get the newsletter out by deadline ("which no one else ever bothers to meet, anyway," I grumbled), I thought about what that radio preacher had said. I mean, here I had listened to his program for years. Why, he was like an old friend—and now I felt betrayed!

His statement had seemed so unfair—and it hurt! I worked just as hard as Rebekah—even if I did use my microwave oven occasionally. Besides, I bet old Isaac didn't have a shiny new tractor to plow his fields and harvest his crops either! So, what about men? Why single us women out anyway?

I left work at noon, still upset, and spent the early part of the afternoon preparing for the back-to-school night and book fair that was scheduled for that evening. By the time I finished that, school was out and my son was home, needing help with his homework, as well as transportation to and from soccer practice.

Somewhere in between all that I got dinner ready (defiantly using my microwave), and then ran out the door to head back to the school. Balancing a cash box, several ledger sheets, my purse and three binders, I fumbled with my keys, trying to unlock the car door.

Hurry, I admonished myself silently. *You're running out of time! Come on, come on!*

Suddenly everything slipped and crashed to the ground, the heavy cash box landing on my foot. As I stood there, my foot screaming in pain, a tiny bubble of laughter began rolling around in my chest. A silly grin tugged at the corners of my mouth, and soon I was laughing out loud.

"Oh, Lord, how ridiculous I am! How could I have let one remark, which had nothing to do with me, ruin my walk with You today? Forgive me,

Lord," I prayed, "and thank You for the gift of laughter! It really puts things back in perspective."

Midway through back-to-school night, a woman came up to me and shook her head. "How in the world do you do it? I mean, you're so organized! Have you ever considered doing workshops on how to manage your time?"

I swallowed a giggle and tried to look serious. "No," I answered. "And I don't water camels either."

As her expression changed from one of admiration to one of total confusion, I added, "But no matter how busy I get, I always make time for laughter."

I winked at her. "Try it. It works wonders — and it'll keep you young forever!"

Adapted from *A Moment a Day* by Mary Beckwith and Kathi Mills (Ventura, Calif.: Regal Books, 1988). Used by permission.

WHO'S IN CHARGE?

WHEN I WAS A KID, I couldn't wait to "grow up and be in charge." I figured that, once I had joined the ranks of those mysterious tall people known as adults, I too could finally do things without checking with someone else first. In other words, I looked forward to that point in time when others were no longer in charge of me, but rather I was in charge of myself—and, if all went well, of a few other people besides.

Well, I made it to adulthood and—surprise! There were still people in charge to whom I was accountable, primarily my boss. But I reasoned that, as soon as I made it through my twenties and thirties and had some seniority on my job, all that would change.

Wrong. Though I no longer have a boss breathing down my neck, since I now work at home, I do still have deadlines to meet. If I don't meet those deadlines, those in charge do not send me any money. (And people wonder where I get my inspiration!)

One of the other misconceptions I had as a child was that, when I had children of my own, they would readily recognize that I was in charge. In essence, I suppose that was true, but I also found that I had to plan my life around the schedules of these little people over whom I was supposed to be in charge. Suddenly, being in charge wasn't all it had been cracked up to be. And by the time the kids were teenagers, I didn't want to be in charge of anything ever again for the rest of my life!

But wouldn't you think that, once I hit that honored position of middle-age and the last of my children is finally at the point of striking out on his own, I should finally be mature enough to be in charge? Well, if you think that, you don't have a pet.

You see, we're cat people. That may come as a

shock to those of you who are dog people because I know there is a distinct dividing line between the two, but cat people we are. And so, Kitty and Weirdo now rule the house. (Only people who are neither cat people nor dog people could fail to understand that statement.)

Every time we settle into our favorite chairs to watch a little TV or do some reading, one of our two felines decides to go in or out. Now, unlike dogs, they do not have a door of their own; consequently, either my husband or I have to get up and open the door for them. At which point, of course, the cat's natural independence surfaces, and Kitty or Weirdo no longer wants in or out. Not until we sit back down, that is.

It's a game they figured out between themselves early on to keep us on our toes—and to remind us daily that the only thing we are in charge of is making sure there's enough cat food in the cupboard to hold them over should a natural disaster strike.

Of course, there are certain things at home that I'm in charge of, whether I want to be or not. For instance, if my husband opens the medicine cabinet and can't find the aspirin, I'm in charge of coming into the bathroom and finding the aspirin by moving the gauze that was in front of the aspirin bottle, hiding it from plain view. If, at any given time, someone in our house is out of matching socks, I'm in charge of washing them, fishing the lost ones out of the dryer vent, or running to the store to buy a new pair, whichever is quickest. And, of course, when my husband becomes incensed over some political travesty and decides that "we should write a letter about that," guess who's in charge?

No, I've decided this "being in charge" stuff is just not for me. So I've made a very wise decision. I've decided to turn everything — and I mean, absolutely everything — over to the One who is really in charge of everything anyway. He does a much better job than I do, and He never gets frustrated over the responsibilities that go with being in charge. And it makes life so much more enjoyable, don't you think?

I LOVE CHILDREN,
BUT NOT IN MY HOUSE

MY FRIEND HAD A BABY the other day. Big deal, you say? Well, considering that she and I are the same age and I already have grandchildren, yes, it is a very big deal. In fact, it is such a big deal that I've been celebrating ever since I heard the news. To be more specific, just before I started dancing on the ceiling I got down on my knees and cried out, "Thank You, Lord, that it's her and not me!"

Oh, I know, the Bible says "children are a heritage from the Lord" (Ps. 127:3). And if God says it, I have no choice but to believe it, do I? But have you ever heard of "inheritance tax"? If you're a parent, you have. You started paying it the moment your little "heritage from the Lord" arrived, and you've been paying ever since. Doesn't matter if your heritage is now five years old or fifty—the payments go on forever.

Now, I didn't know that when I was expecting my first child. In fact, in my naiveté, I thought all babies were born looking just like the Gerber baby, with permanent smiles pasted on their adorable, cherubic faces. And I was not aware that babies never sleep. They only close their eyes and pretend to sleep until their built-in radar informs them that you have just: (a) sat down to dinner; (b) climbed into the shower; (c) turned in for the night. Then, immediately, they begin to scream.

That's another common misconception about babies. People who have never had any think they cry. Trust me. Babies do not cry. They scream. A lot.

Somehow or other though, most of us learn to adapt and, therefore, survive this early stage of parenthood, discovering for the first time that it is indeed possible to live for months on end without sleep. Today's modern mother, however, may be trying to do all of this in addition to maintaining her already-established career. Not to worry though. Today's modern father realizes that it is his responsibility to share in the caretaking of children. Faithfully, he bounds out of bed every fourth Tuesday of every other month to give his new little inheritance a 2 A.M. feeding, leaving his appreciative wife to snooze under the warm covers. Of course, fifteen minutes later when Mom realizes the baby is still screaming, she stumbles out to the kitchen and finds Dad slumped over with his head on the countertop, snoring. The bottle is still in the refrigerator. The screaming baby is still in the bassinette. And Mom is still in charge.

Face it. Some things never change.

But before you know it, that screaming infant becomes a curious little toddler — more commonly known as a "rug-rat" or "curtain-climber." And mind you, there's a good reason for those terms. If you have to ask what it is, you have yet to receive your heritage from the Lord, am I right?

You do have to admit that there's a certain sweetness and charm unique to children of this age. Who else could possibly look cute with strained prunes smeared from cheek to chubby cheek? Which, of course, is the exact time your adorable child is overwhelmed with love for you, forthwith burying his face in your freshly laundered white pants.

However, before you know it, this stage will also pass and your toddler will be embarking on that wonderful journey known as "education." Ever watch parents of kindergartners? You can spot them a mile away—hovering over their precious progeny like so many nervous helicopters.

"Are you sure you don't have to go to the bathroom, sweetheart?"

"Here, darling, let me wipe your face."

"Button your jacket, honey."

"Be sure and drink all your milk, dear, and please don't use the straw to blow bubbles through your nose."

But all that changes, I promise. By the time little Einstein has worked his way up to the fifth grade and Mom and Dad have made 12,000 emergency cupcake deliveries as well as "helped out" on several exciting field trips to the lemon-packing plant and the LaBrea Tar Pits, the teacher couldn't get a volunteer room-parent if she offered free trips to Tahiti with the movie star of your choice!

None of this, however, even begins to prepare you for what comes next. As a matter of fact, combat training with the Green Berets wouldn't be enough. But prepared or not, it arrives—along with ringing telephones, acne attacks, blaring music with lyrics adults can't possibly understand (and would have heart failure if they could), mood swings, broken hearts, $150 tennis shoes, and driver's ed.

That's right. Teenagers. The only self-proclaimed omniscient people on earth. Neither fish nor fowl, these formerly adorable children who once sat on your lap and thought you walked on water, now expect you to pay all of their expenses while at the same time remaining invisible. (There is nothing more embarrassing for a teenager than to be seen in the company of a parent. Definite social-suicide.)

Still, in spite of it all, we love them—most of the time. And let me assure you, even this stage shall pass. Your teenagers will eventually turn into young men and women whom you may be pleasantly surprised to discover that you actually like. However, if you think you're through paying inheritance tax once they're grown and gone, guess again. You still agonize over your children's every sorrow, try to solve their every problem, worry about every twist and turn in their lives.

But just when you think you'll never be able to let go, you hear about someone like my friend with the new baby. And you wonder, How does she do it? I know I don't have the strength or the patience or the energy I had when my children were young. Nor am I prepared to make the obvious adjustments required for having a little one in my home again.

You know what I mean. Getting used to tiny handprints on the coffee table and sliding glass doors. Storing all breakables at shoulder level or above. No light-colored furniture, draperies, or carpets. Definitely no leftover Gravy Train in the dog's dish!

No, I couldn't do it. I'm just too old. Besides, I paid my dues and now I've earned my freedom, right? Why, just the thought of having little ones in my house again....

Wait a minute, who am I kidding here? I have so many pictures of my children and grandchildren on my walls that I'll never have to worry about new paint or wallpaper. And when I dig out my countless photo albums and begin to reminisce, I know that I am reliving the most precious memories any woman could ever have.

Taking the time to reflect on those memories, I realize that my responsibility extends beyond my own children and grandchildren. I have a responsibility to support my friend and her new baby in prayer. Because, regardless of her age, she has just been called to the greatest task any human being can ever undertake: that of raising up another human being, made in the image of God, to know and love and serve God above all else.

Is it worth it? Definitely. Every sacrifice, every inconvenience, every sleepless night. And yes, if called on by God to do it again, I would . . . *however,* until then, I will be more than happy to do my part in praying for those who, even now, are busy loving their precious heritage from the Lord.

I DIDN'T RECOGNIZE YOU WITH YOUR CLOTHES ON

HAVE YOU EVER HEARD of those contests where the winner is the one who can come up with his or her most embarrassing moment? Well, I have, and if I ever hear of another one, I'll enter because I know I'll win, hands down.

It all started out innocently enough. (At my age, what did you expect?) For about two years, I had been going to a gym and, although it was coed, my aerobics class was all women. (You didn't think I'd go anywhere in one of those dumb little workout outfits if there were going to be men there, did you?)

There was, however, one exception. Clyde (not his real name, for soon-to-be-obvious reasons), several years younger than I, was the only male employee at the gym. He was such a permanent fixture I hardly noticed him anymore once I'd been going there for a while.

Throughout the time I attended the gym, I don't remember ever having seen Clyde anyplace else in town, so I was surprised to see him walk into the bank one Friday afternoon. Waiting (along with what seemed to be about a million other people) to cash a check for the weekend, I was next in line for the first available teller when Clyde walked in. He spotted me, did a double take, then started walking my way.

"Kathi," he said, grinning from ear to ear. "I wasn't sure it was you at first. I didn't recognize you with your clothes on."

Ever see the commercial where, when E.F. Hutton speaks, everyone else stops and listens? If so, you know just what happened in the bank that day. You could have heard a pin drop. As I stood there, turning eight shades of crimson and wondering whether I would make the situation worse by trying to explain to everyone that he was referring to the fact that the only other place he had ever seen me was at the gym in my workout outfit, I decided the best thing to do was to forget about cashing my check, run out the door, jump into my car, go straight home, pack a suitcase, and leave town— forever.

Well, I did everything but pack a suitcase and leave town, but I will admit this—I changed banks, and I didn't renew my membership at the gym that year. I told myself it was because the interest rates were better at the new bank and it was cheaper to use one of my aerobic tapes at home, but . . . well, I think you understand.

That incident reminded me of another humiliating time in my life, one that actually was much more serious. I had been a Christian for several years but, for some time, had sort of been "cruising" with the Lord. Know what I mean? Not backsliding in the obvious sense of the word, but not really moving on with the Lord either.

And then, one day I ran into a coworker at church. She was a first-time visitor, and she came right over to me as soon as she saw me.

"Kathi," she said, "I didn't know you were a Christian!" Immediately, she flushed. "I mean . . . I . . . well, I didn't realize you attended this church."

I forced a smile, explaining that I had been coming to the church for quite some time. Inside, I was wishing the floor would open up and swallow me. It didn't, of course, but it all worked out all right anyway. Instead of turning and running, as I did at the bank, I realized how careless I had become in my spiritual walk, and I repented immediately.

Isn't it amazing how we categorize and compartmentalize our lives? We wear our workout outfit to the gym, our best dress for church, our blue jeans to work in the yard. But when we "put on the Lord Jesus Christ" (Rom. 13:14), we should keep Him on — all the time.

I had fallen into the trap of being a "Sunday Christian," which might be OK if all I wanted to do was the socially acceptable thing. But Jesus doesn't care if we are accepted by society. He wants us to remember that "He has made us accepted in the Beloved" (Eph. 1:6), and to walk in such a way that we will be recognized by others as belonging to Him.

And so — although I still avoid that bank and gym — I ask the Lord to let His love and light shine through me so strongly that never again will anyone be surprised to learn that I am a Christian.

A COLLECTOR'S ITEM

THERE ARE SEVERAL THINGS that my husband and I enjoy doing together—and several things we don't. Fishing, for instance.

There is nothing my husband likes better than heading out onto the lake, while it is still very cold and very dark, with nothing to keep him company except a bucketful of worms and the hopes of catching his day's limit of trout. I, on the other hand, believe that fishing should be limited to opening a can of tuna. So, fishing remains one of those things that Larry does on his own.

Sort of like my spending the day at the library. I can't imagine anything more pleasant and relaxing. He'd rather stay home and watch a Discovery Channel special on baiting hooks.

But one of the things we both enjoy immensely is antiquing. We could poke around antique stores together for hours, even if we come out empty-handed most of the time. I'll admit, many of the things we come across in secondhand or antique stores are monstrosities, but every now and then we find something that's just right—and we both know it. Our house is full of those just-right items.

My husband carries it a step further though. He collects antique cars. Well, actually, he buys one or two at a time, fixes them up, and then sells them so he can buy another "toy" to play with.

I have to admit, I find this hobby of his a bit comforting—especially as the years go sailing by. It's nice to know that the man who has promised to grow old along with me enjoys old things, that he sees something of lasting worth and quality in them.

At the same time, I do have one concern. Although he is quite tolerant—even enamored—of older things, he has absolutely no patience with rattles. For a guy who can tune out the TV to the point of falling asleep in front of it (he can do the same thing to my voice, by the way), he cannot bring himself to tune out the slightest rattle in a car.

We can be buzzing down the freeway (at slightly over the speed limit, if he's driving), when suddenly he will pull over and start disassembling the car.

"What are you doing?" I ask.

"I heard a rattle," he answers. "I'm not sure where, but I'll find it."

I've actually known him to stuff the car's ashtray full of cotton balls because he thinks it might be the cause of a rattle.

So what does this mean to me? Am I to anticipate being stuffed full of cotton should I develop a rattle? I suppose only time will tell, but as the years progress, rattles do become a distinct possibility.

Well, I'm not going to worry about it. He promised God that he would love me for better or worse, and I think God includes rattles in that promise. So, as I fast approach the point where I too will become a collector's item, I'll rest in the thought that maybe what's left of his hearing will go before I start rattling.

If not, look for me in the nearest antique store.

ELECTION UPDATE

I'LL NEVER FORGET THE FIRST TIME I was old enough to vote. (And no, it was not during the Herbert Hoover campaign.)

I was so excited. In fact, I really got into it—especially the Presidential race. I saw my candidate as the great reformer, the answer to our country's woes, the "people's choice." Apparently the people didn't agree with me, because he lost by a landslide.

Immediately, disillusionment set in. At the height of the "flower children" era, I decided that politics was definitely not going to bring about the "peace and love" that those of us just coming of age dreamed about.

Looking back, however, I'm glad for that experience of disillusionment. It made me focus on the emptiness I felt inside; in turn, I began to wonder if I would ever discover the answer to having that emptiness filled.

Well, suffice it to say, I did—and not too long after my disillusionment set in, I might add. The answer, of course, was Jesus Christ. He filled all the emptiness with a lasting peace and joy that I wouldn't trade for anything.

But you know what I found out? Jesus isn't running for King—He's already been elected by a majority of One. And you know what else? There's nobody running against Him. But the incredible thing is, we still get to vote—not for whether or not He becomes King, but for whether or not we will be a part of His kingdom.

Wait. It gets even more incredible. The mind-boggling part of all this is that there will be no other kingdom than His, and yet the majority of people still vote against their only option. I mean, maybe if it were going to be a bad kingdom, I could understand it. But the promise from the King is that the kingdom will be *all* good and *all* loving (just like the King).

161

So why would anyone vote against becoming a part of that kingdom? Simple. Entrance to the kingdom requires an admission of unworthiness to be there, and human nature would rather do anything than admit to unworthiness. Consequently, they opt to "take their chances" and vote no. The sad thing is, their chances are zero. In an already-decided election, a no vote is futile.

But on top of all this, there is yet one more incredible fact here. You see, the King didn't have to give any of us a chance to vote at all, since none of us is worthy of being a part of His kingdom. But He decided that, if we would admit our unworthiness, He would impart His own worthiness to us. Such a deal!

And so, although political elections here on earth continue to alternately encourage and disillusion us, we can rest assured that the outcome of the final election has already been decided — and we win!

WHAT IS THE
NEXT GENERATION
COMING TO?

I'LL ADMIT IT. I was one of those strange children who loved school. Of course, part of the reason for that may have been that I was sick a lot as a child, and therefore missed out on a lot of school. Kids (and adults!) are always more readily attracted to anything they think they're missing out on, rather than something they are compelled to do.

Consequently, while other kids were faking tummy aches and sore throats, I worked very hard at convincing my mother I was healthy enough to go to school. If I woke up in the morning with a fever, I would try to act normal. If my mother noticed my eyes were glassy, checked my forehead, and insisted I felt hot, I would counter with, "I feel fine!

Why don't you check my temperature?" Of course, while she was out of the room, I would take the thermometer out of my mouth and shake it back down to normal. Sometimes it worked; most of the time it didn't, and I had to stay home and be satisfied with doing my homework in bed. When I ran out of homework, my mom would go to the library and get me some books.

Reading was my life. I discovered I could go anywhere, do anything, be anybody, simply by reading a book. To this day, reading is my favorite pastime.

Not so today's youth. Whereas I looked on reading as an exciting adventure, children of today view it as boring, if not cruel and unusual punishment.

Ever have this conversation with your kids?

"I'm bored. There's nothing to do."

"Why don't you go outside and play with one of your friends?"

"Nobody's home, and there's nothing on TV."

"Well, you could always read a book."

"Why? I didn't do anything wrong!"

Punishment. A fate worse than death. Not even

worthy of consideration as a last resort to cure boredom. How sad! And how scary.

I mean, think about it. These same kids — our offspring — who hate to read and can't make change without a calculator are the future of our country. We have raised a generation who worships MTV and doesn't even know in what century (or what country) the Civil War was waged, and yet they'll be voting soon! Even now, some of them are driving cars on the very streets through which we must pass daily. Kids who have no idea how to fill out a job application or balance a checkbook are obtaining driver's licenses with the greatest of ease.

Of course, it wouldn't be fair to imply that all of the next generation fall into this functionally illiterate category. I have met some wonderful exceptions to this rule. But overall, the majority of our youth are moving into adulthood without any of the basic skills to endure, let alone excel.

Is it their fault? I don't believe so. After all, our children do not qualify as baby boomers, and yet they are growing up in a world shaped largely by those of us who make up that category of adults.

Where did we go wrong? Well, I doubt there is enough space in this book to go into all that, but I would venture to say that one of our primary failings as a generation of parents who were supposed to prepare the next generation for real life was that, instead of teaching them to think, we taught them to imitate: TV, movies, music, peers. Why did we do that? Because it was easier. Because it freed us to pursue our own interests. Our kids became low man on our totem pole of priorities, and their lack of brain activity reflects that position.

But even worse than the fact that we, as a generation, have fallen down on our responsibilities to teach our children in intellectual matters, we have failed to teach them about moral issues. Although many of our parents raised us with religious and moral convictions, a large proportion of us boomers chose to reject those convictions. Hence, our own children are growing up in the greatest moral vacuum in the history of our country.

Is it any wonder that our children believe the world runs on batteries? That without electricity, all known life forms would cease to exist? That drugs and alcohol and suicide become more and more attractive and acceptable to them every day?

These are our children. The product of our generation. The most important contribution to our world that any of us will ever make. So why are we devoting so much time to other things? Why can't we reprioritize and put our kids back at the top of the totem pole where they belong?

It won't be easy. And it won't happen overnight or without personal sacrifice. Sometimes, they may even fight us on it. After all, readjusting our priorities means readjustment on their parts as well. Less unsupervised time, more accountability, more submission to authority. Nobody likes that at first. But eventually, I believe they will come to thank us, as they learn about a bigger world, one that does not revolve exclusively around them.

They may even come to the point of looking forward to reading a book or writing an essay or studying to pass a law exam. Most important, they may stop trying to fill the moral vacuum in their lives with cheap substitutes and deadly counterfeits.

And maybe—just maybe—they will be able to look at us baby boomers with a measure of admiration and respect.

GOING ONCE,
GOING TWICE...

UP UNTIL A FEW YEARS AGO, the closest I had come to an auction was to watch one on TV. But then my husband came home from work one evening and told me he had gotten tickets to a fund-raising auction for a worthy charity in town.

"Why?" I asked.

"Why not?" he countered. "After all, it's for a good cause."

"Well, I suppose," I conceded.

"Besides," he added, "my boss gave them to me. He had four tickets and thought we might like to join him and his wife."

Ah, now I understood. Worthy charities aside, we were going to the auction because his boss would be offended if we didn't.

The whole thing took place in a park, with the larger items — cars, boats, motorcycles — set up on the grass outside. The smaller items were displayed on tables spread out around the perimeter of a huge revival-type tent. In the midst of this tent is where we all sat, waiting for the auctioneer to hold up the item we just couldn't live without.

"How about that curling iron?" my husband asked. "We don't want to look cheap, so we really should bid on something. Would you like a curling iron?"

I shook my head. "No thanks. I already have one."

"You don't need a spare?" he asked hopefully.

I shook my head again. "No. And if I do, I can run down to the drug store and get one for under $10."

"Well, keep your eyes open," he said. "There must be something in here we can use."

Item after item passed by. Nothing. At least, nothing that I either needed or wanted. Larry's boss' wife had already bought several items though, and Larry was starting to elbow me in the ribs periodically, glaring at me with that please-don't-make-me-look-like-a-cheapskate-in-front-of-my-boss look. So I decided to take the plunge. The very next item, whether I needed it or not, I was going to get it—and price was no object!

Well, imagine Larry's surprise when the very next item turned out to be the final item of the night—a four-day cruise to Mexico. And sure enough, I started bidding on it. So did several other people, however, so I had to work really hard to get that trip. But when the auctioneer finally called out, "Going once, going twice, sold to the lady with the husband who just passed out on the floor," I knew the trip was mine. (I could only assume Larry had fainted from happiness at knowing that his boss now recognized him as a generous man who readily contributed to worthy causes.)

Whether or not that was the reason, he finally revived and we eventually went on our cruise. Granted, it cost approximately three times as much as if we'd gone down to our local travel agent and booked the trip ourselves, but like I told him, what's money when it's for a worthy cause, and besides, it's tax deductible. (That helped a little.)

Well, in spite of the cost, we had a great time. So great, in fact, that we've decided to take another cruise someday—although my husband has assured me that he will take care of making the arrangements himself.

As for me, I haven't been to any more auctions, but I am listening very carefully to hear God say, "Going once, going twice . . . " because when He says, "Gone!" I'm outta here!

When will that be? Well, no one knows for sure, but I think we can safely say, the time is very close. And I know there is a lot of controversy about when we're going—before the Tribulation? Midway through it? Right at the end?

Personally, I don't care. Because if I've learned anything about God during these almost twenty years I've been serving Him, it's that He's never late. So, as my pastor says, "Jesus and I have an agreement. He comes, I go!"

Won't you join us? It may not be tax deductible, but it's the best offer you'll ever get!

A MAN'S GOTTA DO
WHAT A MAN'S GOTTA DO

EVER WATCH THOSE old black-and-white Westerns where the broad-shouldered hero sweeps the beautiful heroine off her feet — in between running all the bad guys out of town and saving the outlying settlers from renegade Indian attacks?

I have — millions of them. Not because I give a hang about them, but my husband thinks they're great. Nothing excites him more than watching Gary Cooper (for the jillioneth time) walk down Main Street at High Noon to single-handedly take on the greatest gunslingers the West has ever known. (To tell you the truth, I think Larry's mother lied to me; he's not her child at all. He was really raised by a pack of coyotes who lives just outside the OK Corral.)

Overall though, I can handle one or two of those low-budget wonders every now and then. But a full day of Clint Eastwood "Hang 'Em High" specials is where I draw the line.

That and John Wayne. Oh, I know, John Wayne is as American as hot dogs and apple pie. But if offered the choice, I'll take the hot dogs and pie every time.

It isn't that I mind so much the fact that he can jump onto a horse streaking by at 90 mph and then ride it backward for six miles without his hat falling off before catching up with the runaway stage and saving all five of the "little ladies" on board. It's their gratitude that nauseates me. And, of course, his reciprocal graciousness.

"A man's gotta do what a man's gotta do," he explains, without cracking a smile.

By that time, of course, the little ladies are bowled over by his charm and wit, and a contest ensues to see who can capture him first.

I say, who wants him? His idea of romance is to growl at a woman and/or ignore her until she is totally furious with him, and then all he has to do is walk in (covered from head to toe with sweat and grime, of course—a manly characteristic if ever there was one), grab her around the waist, and kiss her—rough and hard. After that he-man show of tenderness, the chastened little lady will follow him to the ends of the earth.

I don't think so. Hot dogs and apple pie aside, this type of behavior is simply not acceptable. And it certainly isn't the way God treats us—or expects us to treat others. In fact, it runs counter to everything God teaches the male and female relationship to be.

Now, it's true that God's Word says that, in the home, "the husband is head of the wife" (Eph. 5:23). That does not, however, indicate that a woman is of any lesser importance than a man. And in studying the life of Jesus on earth, one would definitely have to conclude that He came to liberate women, as well as men.

Aside from the apostles, many of Jesus' closest and most trusted companions were women. They loved Him deeply, almost as deeply as He loved them. And they were loyal. When Jesus was dying on the cross and many of His male disciples had deserted Him, Matthew 27:55 tells us that "many women who followed Jesus from Galilee, ministering to Him, were there looking on from afar." It was also women who, inspired by devotion to their recently departed Lord, went to the tomb to anoint His body with spices, only to discover that He was no longer there, but had risen.

Many of us women of baby boomer age grew up with images of men like John Wayne, ordering women around and making brilliant but obviously manly statements such as, "A man's gotta do what a man's gotta do." For that very reason, the feminist movement grew mightily during our lifetime.

But I'm here to tell you, freedom and liberation will not be found in the militant feminist movement of today any more than it is in relationships with guys who pound their chest and swing through trees to prove they're men.

If you really want to be a liberated woman, go to the foot of the cross and look up at the One who knew the real meaning of the words, "A man's gotta do what a man's gotta do"—and then carried them out.

For you.

I OWE IT ALL
TO CLEAN LIVING

WE'VE ALL READ STORIES of people who lived to be 103 and who, when interviewed, credited their longevity to good, clean, healthy living. Others, however, totally blow this theory out of the water.

You know who I'm talking about. The guy in his late 90s who gets married for the eighteenth time, smokes two packs of cigarettes daily, and drinks a case of beer for breakfast. Or my husband's great aunt, who lived to be well over 100 and ate bacon and eggs for breakfast every day of her life. (Of course, I always tell my husband, "You see? I knew that cholesterol would catch up with her sooner or later!")

And then there are those of us who faithfully

count calories, fat grams, glasses of water con-
sumed, and miles walked daily. We wouldn't
dream of eating anything that wasn't marked
"light" or "fat-free." And we buy so many greens
at the grocery store, people in the checkout lines
think we raise rabbits. Not only do we not drink or
smoke, we refuse to sit in the smoking sections of
restaurants. We never cross the street if the sign
says "Don't walk," and we drive six miles to return
too much change to the store clerk.

So does all this mean we will live to be 100?
Erma Bombeck doesn't think so. In fact, she's sure
that if the day comes when she passes up a jelly
doughnut, she'll walk outside and step in front of
a truck.

And yet, something deep down inside tells us
that these are the right things to do—whether we
die at 105 or 45 (which, for me, would have to be
almost immediately) or even 25. Would I feel
cheated if, after doing all these right things, I were
to die what some people consider a premature
death? Good grief, no! How could someone who
knows beyond a shadow of a doubt that "to live is
Christ, and to die is gain" (see Phil. 1:21) ever feel

cheated about anything? At the same time, I believe that if I seek to honor my Lord in the way I live every aspect of my life, then I will not die a premature death. I will remain here just as long as God has purposed for me to serve Him on this earth.

Will I have missed anything by dedicating myself to good, clean, healthy living? Well, maybe. Could be I'll miss out on being a poor example to others, on spending time in a drug or alcohol rehab center, on experiencing certain aspects of poor physical health, or the embarrassment of getting caught in something dishonest or illegal or immoral. And who knows? Maybe I'll even miss out on a jelly doughnut right before I make my final exit. But whether I do or not, one thing I know: Someday I'll have to stand before God and account for what I did with whatever amount of time He gave me to serve Him. True, He probably doesn't give out rewards for sitting in the nonsmoking section of restaurants or keeping cholesterol levels down, but I do believe He will honor us for the times we chose to honor Him—especially when it would have been so much easier to go the other way.

The Apostle Paul tells us in Romans 12:1 that our bodies are to be "living sacrifices" to God, which is our "reasonable service." Therefore, it goes without saying that to do any less would be unreasonable. Have you ever had to deal with an unreasonable child? (Anyone who has lived long enough to be classified as a baby boomer and who has had children should qualify in this area.) I don't know about you, but I don't want my Heavenly Father to have to deal with me as I have had to deal with my own unreasonable children.

So I believe I will continue to do the reasonable thing and listen to that voice down deep inside that tells me to do the right thing—whether or not the world mocks me for doing so, whether or not visible rewards are forthcoming—or whether or not I live long enough to pass up that last jelly doughnut.

THERE'S NO MAYONNAISE
IN IRELAND

SOME YEARS AGO I remember reading an article about a man who was hard of hearing. When
his family said to him something along the lines of
"How are you feeling today?" he thought they had
said, "There's no mayonnaise in Ireland."

I found the article somewhat amusing, but had
no idea how close to home it would someday
come. But close it is! First of all, there's my father.
Now Dad definitely qualifies as a senior citizen
and has for quite some time. Overall, he's in pretty
good health for his age — except for his hearing.

I'll never forget one day when we took Mom
and Dad for a ride. They were visiting us for two
weeks, and we'd noticed how much worse Dad's
hearing had become since their last visit. We had

come to the point where we had to yell in order for him to hear us—or just plain give up and not talk to him. Because we love him, we tried to compensate by permanently raising our volume when we spoke.

Anyway, there we were, riding along and enjoying the scenery, with Larry, Mom, and me talking at a relatively high decibel rating, assuming we were talking loudly enough for Dad to hear us. Apparently we weren't, though, because when we asked him a question regarding the topic we'd been discussing for the previous five minutes, he just blinked and said, "Hamburger?"

Now, I'll admit, his comment may have had something to do with the fact that it was fast approaching lunchtime, but since this was hardly an isolated incident, we knew better.

My parents live out in the country in southwestern Washington. My youngest brother, Jerry, and his family live on the five acres behind them. Naturally, they visit back and forth quite often. One summer evening, Jerry had stopped by just as Dad was watching the news on TV. Jerry was interested in hearing what was going on, but the TV volume was so loud, he couldn't stand being in the house. So he took a chair out onto the front porch, left the door open, and watched and listened to the news from a safe vantage point.

Now, although I have inherited some of my father's characteristics, being hard of hearing is definitely not one of them. What I lack in eyesight, I more than make up for in acute hearing. (My husband says I can hear a mosquito buzzing down the street two blocks away.) He, on the other hand, although not directly related to my dad, may very well be following in his footsteps as far as being a prime candidate for a hearing aid.

This, of course, was not a problem before we got married. "Huh?" was not even in his vocabulary then; now it's become his favorite word. (How much of that has to do with progressive hearing loss and how much with selective hearing loss I'm not sure.) Anyway, he is resisting having his ears checked for hearing aids because, as he says, "It's just one more admission that I'm getting old. Besides, they look stupid." (We all know how brilliant people look who go around saying "huh" all the time, right?)

But I think God is much more concerned with our

spiritual ears than He is with our natural ones. After all, how many times in the Bible does He say, "He who has ears to hear, let him hear!" (Mark 4:9) With the Holy Spirit living inside us as a result of the new birth, God has given us spiritual ears to enable us to hear what God is speaking to us. We, however, must be willing to listen — and obey.

Jesus, in talking about those who believe on Him, said, "They will hear My voice" (John 10:16). More importantly, He said, in referring to Himself as the Shepherd, "The sheep follow him, for they know his voice" (v. 4).

It's not enough just to hear His voice — although we must have ears to hear in order to do even that. But we must also recognize His voice and then follow Him. That is why it is so important to spend time with Him daily, reading His Word and praying, listening to and becoming familiar with His voice.

Because, you see, although there may be no mayonnaise in Ireland, there is perfect hearing in heaven — no matter whether you're a baby boomer or a senior citizen. He wants to give us ears to hear. Receive them.

And then listen.

OH, THE NIGHTLIFE!

IF THERE'S ANYTHING that marks the passing of time more than our change in attitude of what we consider "nightlife," I don't know what it is.

Seriously, I can remember, as a teenager, kicking and screaming because my parents set what I considered unreasonable curfews. I mean, how could anyone possibly have a good time when you had to be in before midnight?

Now I can't even remember the last time I made it up 'til midnight to see in the New Year! When my husband and I talk about going out for a "night on the town," it means we have a coupon for our favorite restaurant's "early bird special."

Up until the time my youngest child reached the age where he could not only tell time but be trusted with a watch of his own (which hasn't been too long ago), the rule was to come home immediately when the streetlights came on. Somehow, that rule seems to have carried over to my husband and me because, invariably, by the time those lights come on, we're home from our evening out, sitting in our favorite chairs, dressed in our pajamas, watching TV or reading. However, if you've recently found yourself sitting in front of the TV in your pajamas at 7 P.M., don't panic. This is not absolute proof that you've reached middle-age. But if you find yourself looking forward to that sort of night-life, your days are numbered!

For instance, where you once looked forward to going to dinner and a late movie on Friday night, do you now find yourself heating up leftovers and browsing through the *TV Guide* to see what time the "Green Acres" and "Get Smart" reruns start? Do you get upset with trick-or-treaters who ring your doorbell after 8:30 P.M. because you have to get out of bed to answer it? Has summer become your least favorite season because the sun doesn't go down as early as you do? Definite warning signs. And they all apply to me.

And yet, deep down, I don't feel like I'm miss-

185

ing a thing. Which, of course, is what it's all about. When I was young (which sometimes seems like yesterday, sometimes like a hundred years ago), I wanted to see and do and learn and experience — and there never seemed to be enough time for it all. But more than that, I really did sense that something was missing in my life, and by staying busy and "having fun" I hoped to either find it or ignore it.

Well, I couldn't ignore it but I did find it — or should I say, it found me. And what it was that I found, that mysterious something that I, along with everyone else in the world, was so desperately searching for, was a love relationship with my Heavenly Father. It's what we were all designed for. Therefore, nothing else can fill the void. And until that void is filled, satisfaction and joy and peace and contentment will continue to elude us.

Of course, I don't mean to imply that, once that void has been filled by God's love, everyone will react by coming home at 7 P.M. each night to put on their pajamas and watch "Leave It to Beaver." But I will say this. When the peace and contentment of God's love has filled your life, you won't

need to spend all your time and energy and resources going to the ball in a pumpkin coach and
dancing the night away in glass slippers. Because
you'll know that your Prince has already come—
and that He's coming again to take you home with
Him! What nightlife could possibly compare with
that?

So settle down in your favorite chair and get out
a good book, or flip on an "I Love Lucy" show.
While everyone else is out spending their money
and missing out on a good night's sleep, you've got
the best seat in the house!

DO YOU HAVE A PLAN B?

FROM THE TIME I WAS A LITTLE GIRL, I practiced the rule, "Always have a plan B." If I woke up one morning, having decided the night before to spend the next day riding my bike, plan B amounted to, if it rains I'll play paper dolls in the house.

As I got older, plan B continued to be a way of life for me. If I had a crush on the guy who sat in front of me in geometry class but he failed to ask me to the dance, I made sure people knew I never could stand him anyway, but I really liked the guy in Spanish II who ended up asking me to the dance after his girlfriend broke up with him. (I'm not sure if anyone bought my story but at least I felt a little better.)

But Plan B really went into action when I had kids. That's when I learned the truth about "The best laid plans. . . . "

It never fails. Get up early and rush around, getting yourself ready before the kids wake up. Then, once they're up, feed and dress them and run for the door, ready to rush off to your appointment on time for a change. And then—you guessed it. Junior gets sick and throws up all over himself. Without a plan B at that point, you're in trouble.

And so we go through life thinking that, as tough as things might get, we've always got options. Somehow, some way, we can always come up with an acceptable alternative.

But you know what? That's just not true. At least, not when it comes to the most important part of life itself. Which is, of course, what happens to you once you die.

Did you know there's no plan B to get into heaven? God gave one plan—plan A—take it or leave it. And yet people continue to insist on trying to come up with a plan B, as if their plan is going to be superior to God's.

Isn't that the height of arrogance? God's plan says, You'll never make it; let Me do it for you. Our plan says, No thank You; I'd rather do it myself. God's plan says, My Son, Jesus, is "the way, the truth, and the life. No one comes to the Father except through" Him (John 14:6). Our plan says, Jesus won't do; there must be another way, and I am bound and determined to find it.

And so, in an effort to disprove the Truth, we go to the most bizarre extremes imaginable, worshiping everything from visions to health foods to money to self. But the One who rules and reigns over the universe still says, "There is no plan B."

Won't you quit striving to do what for you is impossible and let Him to whom nothing is impossible take care of it for you?

RIDING THE RAILS

I HAVE TO ADMIT, I'm not real adventurous. I used to be—when I was young—but now I much prefer comfort to adventure.

Nowhere is this more visible in my life than when it comes to travel accommodations. As a kid, I would have thought nothing of traveling across the entire country on the bus. Now I'm upset if I have to change planes en route to my destination!

You'd think I'd be made of much heartier stuff, considering my father came over to this country in 1929—at the age of 18, *alone*. And chances are, the ship he traveled on did not offer him a deluxe suite.

My mom, on the other hand, was born in this country, but left New York in 1946 to travel—

alone — to the West Coast. As the train snaked its way through the Midwest, dragging along for what seemed like forever just to get across Texas, she admits to having serious second thoughts.

Now, lest you think I've never braved a train ride, think again. In fact, I had always imagined riding the rails to be a very romantic way to travel. And so, a few years ago, we decided to forgo flying or driving and take our annual vacation via Amtrak.

Of course, I had visions of our own little sleeping room all to ourselves, complete with curtains on the window, a couch that folded down into a bed, a private bath. . . . Wrong again. My husband had other ideas.

"A private room?" he asked, grabbing his heart. "Do you know how expensive a private room is? Besides, we're only going to be on the train for twenty-seven hours each way. Surely you can sleep sitting up for just one night!"

Oh, sure. No problem at all. I mean, who couldn't sleep sitting up, while people talk, babies cry, children scream, and conductors walk through the coach all night, shining their flashlights in your

192

face to see if you're asleep.

Aside from that though, the trip wasn't really too bad. Of course, the romantic part went out the window as soon as I found out we were riding in coach with everyone else, so I figured we might as well take our youngest son along.

Chris was excited and spent most of the trip running from car to car, annoying the other passengers and asking us for money for snacks. We gave it to him just so we wouldn't have to keep playing checkers with him in an effort to entertain him each time he sat down to rest from running through the train.

As for saving money though, forget it. Between Chris' snack money and what it cost us for meals, it would have been cheaper to fly. However, for me it wasn't a total washout, because I spent every spare minute reading.

My husband just couldn't understand that. "Why would you want to take a train ride and then spend the whole time with your nose in a book?" he asked. "You're missing all this wonderful scenery."

Right. Trains pass through miles and miles of

nothing, I guarantee you, and when they do come into a town, it's not exactly the scenic route. Primarily, they travel through everyone's backyard which, if you're into looking at other people's laundry hanging on the line, is OK. And, of course, don't forget that for a large portion of that twenty-seven hours, it was dark outside.

Well, the upshot of the whole thing was that, by the time we arrived at our destination, we were all so cranky and exhausted from not getting any sleep that my husband finally agreed to upgrade our return tickets and get that nice little private sleeping room I'd been dreaming about all along.

Which, I'll admit, made the trip home much more enjoyable. We actually did get some sleep, but we still had to play checkers with Chris and give him snack money and pay a week's salary for a hamburger. So, overall, it's a safe bet we'll not ride the rails again—not only because we can't afford it, but because I'm quite sure Amtrak, thanks to Chris, has us on the list of "never again" customers.

Let me explain. If you've never seen one of those private rooms on the train, let me explain to you that the bathroom is tiny. Very tiny. So tiny that the shower and toilet are in exactly the same spot—you just stand or sit, as the case may be. And, on the wall right next to the shower and toilet are two buttons—one marked "Shower" and one marked "Toilet." Just before disembarking the train, Chris switched the signs. (I'll leave the rest to your imagination.)

Now we've all pretty much come to the conclusion that anyplace that takes more than three hours to get to, we fly. Not nearly as adventurous, I'll admit. But much more convenient—and a whole lot cheaper and safer!

I guess I just have to face it. I've reached an age where the only adventure that holds any attraction to me anymore is moving on into eternity. Heaven will be exciting, I know—one great adventure after another. But I won't have to sleep sitting up or play endless games of checkers or pass out snack money.

One thing I know for sure though: I'm going to book my trip in advance so that when the Conductor yells, "All aboard!" I'll be sure to get a seat!

A FAMILY RESEMBLANCE

HAVE YOU EVER NOTICED, the first thing people do when they see a new baby is try and decide who he looks like? Of course, the child never looks exactly like anyone else, since children are offspring, not clones. But before a child is five minutes old, all the relatives have decided that he has Aunt Mable's eyes, Grandpa Homer's nose, Mom's lips, Dad's chin, and Uncle Hiram's hairline (meaning, he is bald as a cue ball).

In our family, I have had the dubious honor of hearing that two of my precious grandchildren, Mikey and Brittney, have my toes. Now, I'm not going to say that my toes are long, but I will admit that, if I had toeless feet, I would wear a size 5 shoe, rather than a size 8. However, I have long since decided (and announced to our entire family) that long toes are a sign of intelligence; therefore, Mikey and Brittney are obviously destined for intellectual greatness.

I'll never forget the time my friend, Shirley, told her three-year-old daughter, Julie, that she had her Aunt Cecelia's eyes. Now, Aunt Cecelia lived almost 3,000 miles away and she and Julie had never met. But as soon as Julie heard this news, she started to cry.

"What's the matter, honey?" Shirley asked her distraught daughter.

"I'm sorry," Julie sobbed. "I didn't mean to take Aunt Cecelia's eyes. Now she can't see!"

Which goes to show, our children don't really have anyone's eyes or ears or smiles other than their own. They are individuals who may or may not resemble their relatives. But one thing is sure: They are made in the image of God, just like everyone else. However, that image is marred due to the sin nature with which each of us is born. The only way to "unmar" our image is to be born again—with a new nature, a sinless nature, inherited from God.

At that point, we really do begin to resemble our Heavenly Father. In fact, the Bible says that, once God has begun a good work in us through new birth, He will complete that work (see Phil. 1:6). And just what is that work? Well, 2 Corinthians 3:18 explains it this way: "But we all, with unveiled face, beholding as in a mirror the glory of the Lord, are being transformed into the same image from glory to glory, just as by the Spirit of the Lord."

God is changing us from glory to glory into the likeness of Jesus. How does He do that? As we look into His Word (the mirror) and read and apply it in our lives, the Spirit of the Lord living inside us makes that Word flesh, and we begin to resemble Him more and more.

When will the work be done? When He returns and we finally see Him face-to-face, as 1 John 3:2 explains: "Beloved, now we are children of God; and it has not yet been revealed what we shall be, but we know that when He is revealed, we shall be like Him, for we shall see Him as He is."

Have you ever heard people say that a husband and wife who have been married for many years begin to look alike? Or how an adopted child takes on more and more of his adoptive family's characteristics and attributes until, one day, he looks like a natural-born child, rather than an adopted one?

That's how it is with us. The more time we spend in fellowship with our Heavenly Father, reading His Word and praying, allowing the Holy Spirit to change us accordingly, the more we begin to resemble our Heavenly Father. And if you're wondering what the Father looks like, remember that Jesus is the "express image" of the Father (Heb. 1:3), and that Jesus said, "He who has seen Me has seen the Father" (John 14:9).

But the work won't be finished until Jesus comes back. Then, when we see Him, we will really be like Him. In fact, we will be one with Him and with the Father, fulfilling Jesus' prayer in John 17:21.

The Family resemblance will finally be complete.

AND THEY LIVED
SAPPILY EVER AFTER

I SUPPOSE IT GOES WITHOUT SAYING that I love to write, and people who love to write usually love to read. I am no exception. One of the first things I ask my students when I start teaching a writing course is, "How many books do you read each week?"

Of course, most of them are sure I made a mistake and meant "How many books do you read each month?" or even "each year." But I mean exactly what I said—each *week*. It is beyond my imagination how anyone could aspire to write if they are not first an avid reader. And by avid, I mean reading a minimum of between one and three average-length books per week (in addition to Bible reading, assigned study reading, etc.).

Because that's what I do. I devour books and magazines the minute I get my hands on them. Although I subscribe to only three magazines on a regular basis, I read them all from cover to cover within two to three days of receiving them in the mail. When people ask me whether I prefer reading fiction or nonfiction, I reply, "Whichever I happen to be reading at the moment."

There is one exception, however. Romance books. Oh, I know, I shouldn't be closed minded, and I really have tried reading them, now that the Christian market has begun producing several lines of them and you don't have to worry about hiding your head in shame while reading them. But I still can't get excited about them. I mean, with few exceptions, I know exactly how the book is going to turn out before I finish chapter 2.

One thing I must say in their favor, however, is that I'd certainly rather believe the picture of love and romance painted by Christian authors than that portrayed on TV soaps and sitcoms. Still, I tend to get a bit bored with the repetitious "And they lived sappily ever after" endings.

But you know what? I once decided I was being

unfair in my assessment of this particular genre, so I attempted to write one of my own. Didn't turn out very well though. And I'll tell you why. I was trying to write the type of book that I simply did not enjoy reading. In short, my heart wasn't in it — and the results reflected that.

One of the first things you learn in writing is to "write what you know." Well, I'm forty-something, am happily (not sappily) married, and have a whole slew of kids and grandkids, so I know at least a little something about romance. But I think there's more to writing than just writing about what we know. I believe we should write about what we love.

Think about it. We talk about the things we love — our family, our job, our hobbies, our causes, our country, our world, our Lord, ourselves — and reveal much of our maturity and caring levels in the process. So it stands to reason that we should write very specifically about those same things. And, although I love my husband and enjoy the romance we share, I do not love nor do I enjoy reading romance books. Therefore, I guess I should just step back and leave that sort of writing for those who do (and who do it so much better than I).

But, because that still leaves me with such a wide variety of both fiction and nonfiction books that I enjoy reading, it follows that I also have a wide variety of types of books to write. Yet, no matter whether I write humor or fiction or nonfiction or poetry, for adults or for children, I find myself writing about the same message — that "God so loved the world that He gave His only begotten Son, that whoever believes in Him should not perish but have everlasting life" (John 3:16).

I suppose the reason for that is, of all the things I have ever read, nothing has more deeply affected me than that message of the love that gave everything — for me. I received that love for the first time at the age of twenty-six, long before crossing that line into middle-age where I now reside. I have dedicated the rest of my life — however long it may be — to bringing that same message of love to others. It is not a "sappily ever after" message, but it is one of unfailing, unending, undeserved love.

If you've never received that love, do so now. God has never regretted giving it. You'll never regret receiving it. And I'll never regret telling you about it.

LIFE AFTER DAYTIME TV

THERE ARE A LOT OF THINGS in this world that concern me, including the unsaved, the homeless, abortion, nuclear wars, and racial prejudice, just to name a few. But there's something else that I have recently added to my list, and I think maybe it needs to be right up there at the top, next to the skyrocketing price of ketchup.

Daytime TV. To be more specific, the people who watch daytime TV. And obviously there must be quite a few, because these bizarre programs are thriving.

Soap operas, of course, are the most obvious. I can only assume that people watch them because their own lives are so dull that they feel they must live vicariously through some daily thirty-minute fix, during which the young, beautiful starlet gets married (for the fifth time in less than two years) to her dead brother-in-law, who really wasn't dead after all, but had just been wandering around the North Pole with amnesia since his motorcycle accident. Of course, the starlet isn't really who everyone thinks she is; she is actually her long-lost identical (but evil) twin, who has kidnapped her sister and is hiding her out in the attic of the hospital — which, of course, is where everyone else on the program works.

Now there was a time when soap opera viewers were comprised almost exclusively of what would now be considered baby boomer age women. Not so anymore. Some men have become hooked, as well as large numbers of teenagers!

But it isn't just soaps that have these people addicted. Soap operas' major competition is now the controversial talk shows. What even soaps can't portray (which isn't much) on TV, is flaunted openly on these egotistical, self-seeking, televised confrontations, such as "Live with Juana Bett!"

Ms. Bett comes strutting out on stage trying her best to look sophisticated yet "homey" (I didn't say "homely"), culturally elite yet just-plain-folks. Her guests for the day are three married couples, each of whom has survived repeated murder attempts by their respective spouses. And yet, love has triumphed and they have stayed together. Before the show ends, however, it may very well turn into a free-for-all combination of "Murder, She Wrote" and "Divorce Court."

Intellectually stimulating? Not at all. Morally uplifting? No way! Socially redeeming? Not a chance. Yet people tune in, day after day. And, although as I stated earlier, not all viewers are baby boomer aged women, a large percentage are.

That concerns me. We are the generation who has grown up, for the most part, with a silver (or at least a bronze) spoon in our mouth. Our parents wanted us to have all the things they missed out on, especially during the Depression. Few of us have suffered any real and lasting poverty. And yet, when it comes to wise use of our time, many of us baby boomers (both men and women) are mentally and morally bankrupt.

OK, you're right. I'm beginning to sound more than a bit critical and judgmental. And I certainly don't mean to pick on those whose lives have come to revolve around other peoples' joys and/or miseries, via soaps and talk shows. But face it, daytime TV certainly reflects a morally bankrupt lifestyle to a frightening extent.

Now please remember, when I talk about baby boomers, good or bad, I'm including myself. And I can't help but think that ours is the generation that has been so blessed and has so much to offer, and yet, as a rule, we give so little in return.

Unlike our parents, who worked and saved and scraped for everything they had and yet were known as a giving and generous generation, we who have so much more to give, give so much less. And that's sad.

Especially if we call ourselves Christians. The One we claim as our Lord and God is always a Giver, as evidenced in John 3:16, which says, "For God so loved the world that He gave." The One we have chosen to follow never wasted His time. Instead, He declared, "I *must* be about My Father's business" (Luke 2:49, italics mine).

I believe that is God's call to all of us, regardless of which generation we were born into or whether or not we spend our time watching daytime TV—or anything else, for that matter. If we become givers who are about the Father's business, there won't be any time left to be takers and squanderers of precious moments. And the farce of daytime TV—along with a lot of other worldly distractions—just might find their ratings down and their season canceled—permanently.